ASSESSMENT LITERACY

for Educators in a HURRY

ASCD MEMBER BOOK

Many ASCD members received this book
as a member benefit upon its initial release.

Learn more at **www.ascd.org/memberbooks**

ASSESSMENT LITERACY

for Educators in a HURRY

W. James POPHAM

 | Alexandria, Virginia USA

1703 N. Beauregard St. • Alexandria, VA 22311-1714 USA
Phone: 800-933-2723 or 703-578-9600 • Fax: 703-575-5400
Website: www.ascd.org • E-mail: member@ascd.org
Author guidelines: www.ascd.org/write

Deborah S. Delisle, *Executive Director;* Stefani Roth, *Publisher;* Genny Ostertag, *Director, Content Acquisitions;* Julie Houtz, *Director, Book Editing & Production;* Katie Martin, *Editor;* Judi Connelly, *Associate Art Director;* Donald Ely, *Senior Graphic Designer;* Mike Kalyan, *Director, Production Services;* Shajuan Martin, *E-Publishing Specialist;* Valerie Younkin, *Production Designer*

Cartoons by Jimmy Malone.

PAPERBACK ISBN: 978-1-4166-2648-0   ASCD product #119009

PDF E-BOOK ISBN: 978-1-4166-2650-3; see Books in Print for other formats.

Quantity discounts are available: e-mail programteam@ascd.org or call 800-933-2723, ext. 5773, or 703-575-5773. For desk copies, go to www.ascd.org/deskcopy.

ASCD Member Book No. FY18-9 (August 2018, P). ASCD Member Books mail to Premium (P), Select (S), and Institutional Plus (I+) members on this schedule: Jan, PSI+; Feb, P; Apr, PSI+; May, P; Jul, PSI+; Aug, P; Sep, PSI+; Nov, PSI+; Dec, P. For current details on membership, see www.ascd.org/membership.

Library of Congress Cataloging-in-Publication Data
Names: Popham, W. James, author.
Title: Assessment literacy for educators in a hurry / W. James Popham.
Description: Alexandria, VA : ASCD, [2018] | Includes bibliographical references and index.
Identifiers: LCCN 2018018949 (print) | LCCN 2018023544 (ebook) | ISBN
  9781416626503 (PDF) | ISBN 9781416626480 (pbk.)
Subjects: LCSH: Educational tests and measurements. | Educational evaluation.
  | School improvement programs. | School improvement programs.
Classification: LCC LB3051 (ebook) | LCC LB3051 .P614155 2018 (print) | DDC
  371.26—dc23
LC record available at https://lccn.loc.gov/2018018949

27 26 25 24 23 22 21 20 19 18   1 2 3 4 5 6 7 8 9 10 11 12

PREFACE

My dictionary says that a *preface* is an introduction to a book, "typically stating its subject, scope, or aims." That sounds about right. Accordingly, in this preface, I'll identify the subject, scope, and aims of the book that you are about to read.

I have written a good number of prefaces during my career, and their length varies substantially. This one will be terser than most, because this book addresses significant stuff, vitally important to the teachers and administrators who are our nation's educational professionals, and I want you and every other reader to get to the substance of it without delay.

Let's get the three dictionary-defined tasks for prefaces out of the way. The *subject* of the book is a set of high-priority understandings about educational assessment, understandings that will typically reduce the number and the magnitude of measurement-based mistakes within the world of education. Putting it differently, grasping the six high-priority assessment truths that are the focus of this book will diminish—or eliminate altogether—most of the educational errors triggered by the misuse of educational tests.

Although this book's *scope* is modest, preoccupied with just six understandings, its impact is potentially vast. That's because these understandings are educational assessment's most basic and truly fundamental concepts and procedures. They have direct bearing on the day-in and day-out decisions educators make. These decisions, if made well, will improve the quality of education that our students receive.

Finally, this book's *aim* is easy to isolate: to help readers who are educators become "assessment literate" as rapidly as possible. To be fair, I gave the aim away in the title. The oft-uttered adage "You can't judge a book by its cover" is intended to dissuade folks from reliance on surface factors rather than substance. But whether a not-yet-read book is an espionage novel or a guide to gluten-free dining, the title usually gives a prospective reader a clue or two about the content therein. Such is the case with the book you are currently clutching.

In 2017, Neil deGrasse Tyson published *Astrophysics for People in a Hurry,* a book deftly focused on a set of basic questions about our universe. Because Tyson is a well-known authority who writes with grace and clarity about a fascinating topic, naturally the book scaled the heights of many a best-seller list. And because his identified audience—"people in a hurry"—happens to describe almost every teacher and administrator I know, I thought I might as well pinch that portion of his title. With apologies to Professor Tyson, I believe educational assessment is a whole lot more interesting and relevant to humankind than any stuffy old astrophysics book.

These references to "you" presume I know who *you* are. I don't, of course, but when I decided to tackle this sort of book, the folks for whom I imagined I'd be writing were already on-the-job educators—teachers as well as school-district or school-site administrators. I was convinced that today's educators, most of whom never received formal instruction on testing, needed a short, easy-to-read book covering the fundamentals of educational assessment. The other audience I had in mind was up-and-coming teachers lucky enough to be enrolled in a formal course focused on teaching or testing. If the latter describes you, I'm confident that you'll enter the teaching force positively luminescent with assessment literacy, and the students you'll go on to teach will be all the better for it.

The approach I've taken in this book reflects my own experiences as an educator. After earning a bachelor's and master's degree from a small college, I put in a two-year stint as a high school teacher in rural Oregon. Yet, I've spent most of my life being a college professor. Accordingly, when writing about any topic that seems to call for explanations, my natural inclination is to become annoyingly *professorial* and dish out a flock of explanations as though I were lecturing to a classful of occasionally attentive college students. I have deliberately discarded such a professorial persona for this book. I've tried to frame all explanations as though I were simply chatting with a colleague in a faculty lounge and keep my professorial proclivities—blather-laden habits spawned by decades of professing—in check.

Although not required to do so by my dictionary's terse definition of what a preface is supposed to do, I am herewith seizing the opportunity to thank my ASCD editor, Katie Martin, for her consistently fabulous work in making my words behave properly in all six of the books I have written for ASCD. As always, I owe her my applause and my appreciation.

W.J.P.
July 2018

ASSESSMENT LITERACY

The What, the Why, and the How

This is a book about educational testing, written specifically for the classroom teachers and school and district administrators who keep our schools running. In this very first chapter, I'll tell you what the book is about—and why the topics it treats are so important to me, to you, to your colleagues, and to the entire nation.

As many teachers and administrators did, I chose a career in education because I wanted to help young people learn—individual children, of course, but also children collectively. Although a high-quality education for the individual child is the ultimate goal of schooling, folks who are ambitiously minded think in more macro terms. What we want is a high-quality education for every child. If we are practical as well as ambitious, we try to figure out how to make that a reality. Now, after a lengthy career, I am convinced that the single *most cost-effective way* to improve our nation's schools is to increase educators' assessment literacy.

I suspect that my "most cost-effective" improvement claim might strike you as overstated, but I really think it is stone-cold accurate. To illustrate, if we were somehow able to *double* the salaries of those in the teaching profession, we would soon find flocks of talented young men and women signing up to become teachers; in time, those talented new teachers would have a positive impact on students' learning. Yet, doubling teachers' salaries would cost a nontrivial chunk of change.

Similarly, if we could reduce by half the number of students that each teacher must instruct, the resultant smaller class sizes would likely lead to learning improvements. But, as was true with my salary-doubling fantasy, any meaningfully reduced class-size strategy would be expensive—probably prohibitively so.

It is *because* cost constraints often deter us from taking powerful actions to improve education that I believe a book touting a truly cost-effective strategy to improve our schools deserves attention. Increasing assessment literacy is just such a strategy. It requires no state budget-busting revision of school funding formulas; it only requires educators to learn something new. When *assessment-literate* educators make educational decisions based on appropriate assessment-elicited evidence, the resultant decisions will almost always be more defensible—meaning, more likely to improve students' learning.

That's why the content of this book matters to me, and why I think it should matter to you and to all of us.

Before we dig in deeper, I want to pause for questions. Specifically, here at the outset I want to explore four questions in a way that will provide a framework for the entire book:

1. What is assessment literacy?
2. Why aren't educators already assessment literate?
3. Why should educators become assessment literate?
4. How can an educator become assessment literate?

By the close of this chapter, I hope that you'll have arrived at your own answers to these four questions. Oh, to be sure, I hope your answers will resemble mine, but modest differences are certainly tolerable.

What Is Assessment Literacy?

Here is the definition of assessment literacy that I've been ladling out in my writing for the past two decades:

> *Assessment literacy consists of an individual's understanding of the fundamental assessment concepts and procedures deemed likely to influence educational decisions.*

Because this whole book revolves around the concept of assessment literacy, let's make sure we agree on what the key components of this definition mean.

Which Fundamental Assessment Concepts?

First off, you'll note that the definition centers on an individual's "understandings of fundamental assessment concepts and procedures." What are these fundamentals, anyway?

Well, for openers, we can look at a pivotal term in that phrase: *assessment*. In this book, I'll be following the lead of most educators today who use the terms *assessment, test, exam,* and *measurement* interchangeably. Yes, a few writers attempt to squeeze some subtle distinctions from certain of those labels, but I typically don't. For many adults, of course, the term *test* evokes an image of the paper-and-pencil exams that they were obliged to complete when they were students themselves. Then, too, the label "measurement" often conjures up images of determining distances (from short ones to interstellar ones) or calculating weight (from slight to substantial). Perhaps the avoidance of such preconceptions is why the label "assessment" currently sits atop today's testing-synonyms usage rankings. It is seen to be the most generally applicable descriptor, and it is accompanied by less extraneous or contaminating baggage.

Educational assessment, then, can be used to describe the full range of procedures that we employ to determine a student's status—for instance, how well students can wander in the world of algebra or how skillfully a student can slug it out with science concepts. In the pages to come, if you occasionally find me using the terms *measurement, exam,* or *test* rather than *assessment,* please know that I am not trying to nudge you toward some sort of cleverly nuanced assessment truth. It's more likely that I simply became tired of using the A-word.

But what about the L-word? Assessment literacy is less akin to "literacy" in general—the ability to read and write—than it is to competence and knowledge in a specific arena, such as "wine literacy" or "automotive literacy" or "media literacy." As stated in the definition presented just a few paragraphs ago, the basics of assessment literacy are *fundamental assessment concepts and procedures*—those that are truly foundational. In this setting, *concepts* refer to such measurement notions as validity, reliability, and fairness. *Procedures* refer to the techniques or methods commonly used to build or evaluate tests—for instance, the techniques employed to identify test items that are biased against certain subgroups of test-takers.

Decision-Influencers Only

As you can see, assessment literacy is not centered on just *any* old run-of-the-mill collection of fundamental concepts and procedures; it deals exclusively with the handful of fundamental concepts and procedures *likely to have an actual impact on educational decisions that can change children's lives.*

Although the stakes are high, an encouraging feature of assessment literacy is that it focuses on just the *decision-influencing* basics of educational measurement. Grasping these is an eminently manageable task.

Why Aren't Educators Already Assessment Literate?

After this little bit of delving into the nature of assessment literacy, you might be wondering about the degree to which *today's* educators are familiar with the concepts and procedures of educational assessment you'll be reading about in the pages to come.

It is a good wonder, and it's a suitably timed wonder for this first chapter. Sadly, an enormous number of today's educators are *not* assessment literate. They simply do not understand the fundamental concepts and procedures of educational testing.

Assessment Literacy Initiatives

I'm not the first person to point this out. Governmental groups such as state departments of education and nongovernmental organizations including the National PTA and the National Association of Elementary School Principals (NAESP) have launched numerous initiatives directed toward enhancing the assessment literacy of educators, educational policymakers, students' parents, and even students themselves. But most of those efforts have only been undertaken in recent years, so we are unlikely to see a substantial boost in assessment literacy among these targeted groups any time soon.

At present, many observers conclude that the target audiences most in need of enhanced assessment literacy are the nation's teachers and educational administrators. The more knowledgeable that these pivotal people are about educational testing's basics, the more readily they can share their assessment-related insights with other individuals, such as the school board members who govern our schools or the parents of the students our schools serve.

It has often been said that "a little knowledge is a dangerous thing." As with most such maxims, at least a wisp of wisdom resides therein. When people know a little bit about something, they frequently believe they know more about it than they actually do. Thinking they've acquired all they need to know, they're disinclined to pursue the topic further and, thus, are all too ready to proffer advice well beyond what they should be proffering.

Far too many of our nation's educators are caught in this trap of knowing too little about assessment yet believing it's enough. These are professionals, and many have been so for years. They write tests, formal and informal. They administer tests regularly, both tests of their own design and tests provided by external, expert sources. They look at test results and make decisions about what these results mean. It's all going fine. What could they be missing? What more is there to know?

Problems in the Midst of Progress

We are now beginning to see a meaningful uptick in the number of states that require teachers to complete a formal course in educational measurement during their teacher-education days. *Yet*, and this is a *yet* well deserving of its italicization, many of these teacher-preparation courses are taught by professors who are measurement *specialists*. The courses they design are filled with debatably relevant, sometimes-obscure assessment content. Where they ought to be serving up only the most *decision-influencing* content, they swamp prospective teachers with impractical measurement esoterica. Putting it candidly, at present we can't automatically conclude that a newly minted teacher, even one with an educational measurement course under his or her belt, is actually assessment literate.

Nor are educational administrators immune from the adverse consequences of assessment illiteracy. In many locales, most of the individuals who have completed training to become certificated educational administrators were not required to take even a single course in educational assessment. And if they were, there's a high likelihood that the course they completed was more in line with the technical interests of the measurement maven who taught the course than with the practicalities of how real-world educators should measure the progress of real-world students.

What I am contending here, then, is that it is a profound mistake to assume that the teachers or administrators with whom you interact are, themselves, assessment literate. They may indeed, through no fault of their own, be ill-prepared to make many of the most important instructional decisions they face. They think they know "enough" about assessment, but most of them don't.

An Author's Confession

And just so you don't think I'm using this printed-page platform to belittle my colleagues, I am putting myself right up there near the head of the "He Thought He Knew" queue. You see, when I was preparing to become a high school teacher, I never received *any* meaningful instruction regarding the fundamentals of educational measurement. Exactly three class-sessions of a required educational psychology course I took were devoted to the care and feeding of multiple-choice test items, but this was all that I and my fellow teachers-to-be got.

Thus, when I began teaching my first students, what I drew on to devise my own classroom tests was my recollection of the tests that I had personally taken as a student. Some of those tests were solid; some were shabby. For fully the first half of my career as an educator, I really had nothing to do with educational testing, preferring instead to focus on the instructional side of teaching. Like most, I assumed that I knew "enough" about testing, and that loftier levels of understanding were the provenance of measurement specialists, *psychometricians* specifically trained to successfully wrestle assessment problems into submission.

It was only when test scores began being used to make high-stakes decisions about students and schools—often important and sometimes-irreversible decisions—that I belatedly recognized the significance of testing's impact on teachers' day-to-day instruction. In short, for much of my own career, I was every bit as indifferent to what went on inside the testing tent as are many of today's teachers and administrators. I realize all too well what it is like to be assessment illiterate.

Quickly, about that label—"assessment *illiterate*." It's rare for productive educational conversations to ensue when someone who is less than expert about a topic is described in terms that could be perceived as derogatory or offensive. I have reservations about employing this term and discourage its use. It won't appear in the book beyond this introductory chapter.

Dispensation and a Promise

Because it is likely that you are an educator, I want to take a moment to disabuse you of what might be characterized as "entry guilt." If you are feeling remorse because you are not *already* assessment literate, I'd like to dispel that right now. It's not your fault, and you have plenty of company. Besides, by reading this book, you're putting yourself on the path to where you need to be.

Why Should Educators Become Assessment Literate?

The overriding purpose of this book is to help educators understand a handful of measurement concepts and procedures so that they can apply them properly to make sound instructional decisions and improve the quality of education that their students receive.

Moreover, becoming assessment literate will pay off personally for educators. The more they understand about the basic notions and processes that play a prominent role in educational decision making, the more likely it is that they will opt for the best choice among those decision options they face. These more defensible decisions will benefit the students under their care. They will make educators better educators—and this is something others will notice. Put candidly, if you are assessment literate, the odds increase that you will be *regarded* as a successful educator because—in fact—you *will be* a successful educator.

Making good decisions means avoiding mistakes, and the kinds of mistakes that assessment-illiterate teachers and administrators make fall into three categories: (1) *using the wrong tests*, (2) *misusing results of the right tests*, and (3) *failing to employ instructionally useful tests*. Let's dip into brief explanations and a few examples of these three mistakes right now.

Using the Wrong Tests

One of the most serious mistakes made by educators—particularly influential educators such as district or state superintendents—is to evaluate other educators' instructional success by leaning heavily on the scores students have earned on standardized tests. What you will learn later on in this book is that most of today's standardized tests are accompanied by *no evidence* that those tests are suitable for such an important evaluative mission. Many standardized educational tests provide technical evidence of one sort or another—for instance, how consistent students' scores are when a test is completed at different times during the school year. But those very same standardized tests being used to *evaluate* our schools supply no evidence whatsoever that students' scores can be used to accurately identify teachers' instructional effectiveness. Consequently, the determination of whether particular schools are effective or not, and the resultant decisions on follow-up actions to take or not take, are almost certain to be incorrect.

Thus, we see strong schools, having been incorrectly judged to be weak according to the wrong tests, directed by higher-ups to modify their "unsuccessful" instructional approaches. Or we see truly effective schools forced to abandon methods that are working well for their students because the wrong tests are incapable of detecting the progress students are making. Conversely, we sometimes see weak schools being regarded as strong simply because their students, who come from families sporting a higher socioeconomic status, learned in the home what they are not learning in school. If *appropriate* evaluative tests had been used, such weak schools would be accurately identified, and their instructional shortcomings could be sensibly addressed.

The evaluation of schools and teachers according to students' scores on a test that is flagrantly wrong for the task is a particularly vexing mistake because it is such a readily correctable one. To evaluate the effectiveness of schools or teachers accurately, we simply need to use tests that evidence indicates are appropriate for this evaluative function.

Misusing Results of the Right Tests

A second commonly encountered measurement-related mistake is misapplication—when tests that are appropriate for one purpose are inappropriately used for another purpose. This is a more complicated issue, because there is nothing fundamentally flawed about finding a new use for a test that was developed to serve a different specific purpose. However, we can't automatically assume every educational test is all-purpose. It is *always* necessary to collect convincing evidence that a test built specifically for one measurement mission is suitable for satisfying a different one.

Here is a common illustration of this second kind of measurement mistake. At three different points over the school year, Ms. Miller's 5th grade students complete a 40-minute mathematics test that samples the content to appear on the year-ending standardized mathematics test. Ms. Miller is using an *interim test,* an assessment administered several times during the academic year in slightly different forms (versions) to the same students—usually in the same classroom or, possibly, in all classrooms at the same grade level in a school. Interim tests can be developed by local educators, but these days, such tests are often created and marketed by commercial testing firms.

The specific intention of this test, according to the test's publisher, is to help teachers make "more accurate *predictions* about students' future academic performances." Specifically, students' scores are intended to help teachers like Ms. Miller identify which of her students are likely to pass (or fail) the state's one-hour, end-of-school-year standardized accountability exam in mathematics. To create an interim test that will support accurate predictions of end-of-year test performance, the assessment firm carefully samples the full range of 25 math skills measured by the annual accountability test. However, a consequence of this comprehensive content coverage is that the many of the skills appearing on the end-of-school-year accountability test can be assessed by only one or, at most, two items on each form of the interim test. Given that the test must be completed by 5th graders within a single class period, there's no room to include more.

Fast-forward to Ms. Miller classroom, where the test creators' careful alignment and expert sampling has paid off. For the past few years, each of the three equivalent forms of the interim test have done an accurate job of predicting how well her students will perform on the spring accountability test. Now, in September, with the first set of interim test scores in front of her, Ms. Miller is planning an intervention. She intends to focus her remedial instruction on *each* student's distinctive weaknesses, so she makes a list of which test items each student answered incorrectly and which skills those items sample. In other words, she is making judgments about each student's skill mastery based on that student's performance on the one or two items that correspond to that skill.

She is using a *predictor* test as an instructionally *diagnostic* test—something it was not intended to be.

As we'll explore further in Chapter 3, arriving at a sufficiently accurate inference about a given student's *per-skill* mastery based on that student's performance on *only one or two items* is patently indefensible. It's an example of when an educational assessment that is marvelous for one purpose can easily lead to erroneous educational decisions when it is used for a different purpose.

Failing to Employ Instructionally Useful Tests

During the past two decades, educational researchers have assembled a boatload of convincing evidence leading to an essentially uncontested conclusion: when classroom assessments are employed to monitor students' learning—so that teachers and students can determine whether any adjustments are needed in what's going on—students learn far better than they would otherwise.

Usually referred to as "formative assessment" or "assessment *for* learning," this *instructional* use of educational assessments will be addressed in Chapter 6. Yet, before we get there, I want you to consider a straightforward, double-if-then proposition: *If* there is evidence that classroom assessments, when used as part of the formative assessment process, can emphatically contribute to greater learning by students, and *if* such assessments are *not* being used for such a praiseworthy purpose, *then* we have arrived at our third category of mistaken uses of educational tests.

Assessment-literate educators know the value and use of formative assessment. They tend to make more appropriate decisions about which tests to use to gain insight into students' learning progress and how to employ the results of such tests. Educators who are *not* assessment literate tend to make inappropriate decisions about which tests to use and how to employ test results to improve instruction and learning. Assessment literacy, in short, improves the likelihood that the students we serve will receive a better education. And this, of course, is an aspiration well worthy of our pursuit.

Figure 1.1 illustrates the sequence of events that typically take place when educational decisions are made by assessment *literate* versus assessment *illiterate* educators. As the graphic indicates, the targeted dividend from educators who make more appropriate decisions is the improved education of students. If you ask me, this is the only reason for educators to muck around with measurement in the first place.

FIGURE 1.1 | Consequences of Assessment Literacy and Illiteracy

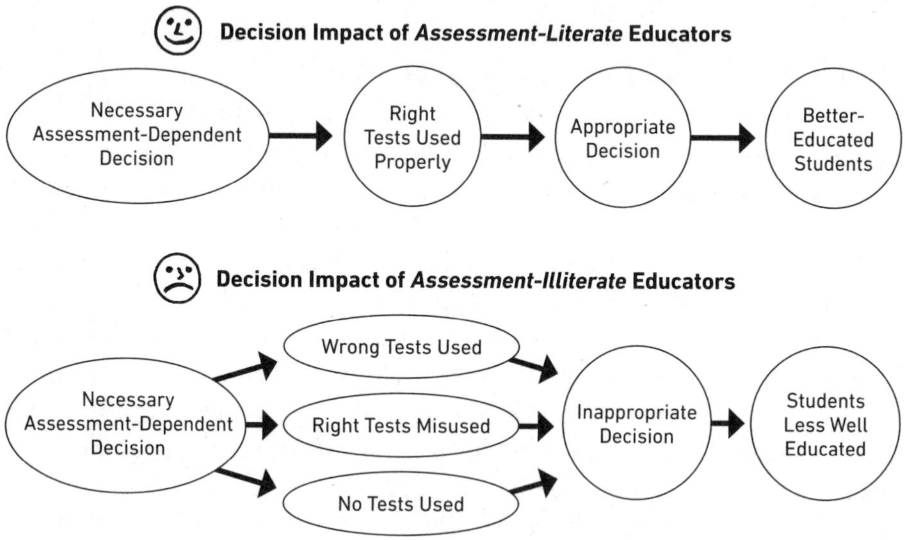

😊 Decision Impact of *Assessment-Literate* Educators

Necessary Assessment-Dependent Decision → Right Tests Used Properly → Appropriate Decision → Better-Educated Students

😠 Decision Impact of *Assessment-Illiterate* Educators

Necessary Assessment-Dependent Decision →
- Wrong Tests Used
- Right Tests Misused
- No Tests Used

→ Inappropriate Decision → Students Less Well Educated

How Can an Educator Become Assessment Literate?

The fourth and final question to be addressed in this opening chapter deals with how to cope with the current reality in which many more teachers and administrators need to become assessment literate. Perhaps, if you wish to personalize this question just a smidge, you might think of it as how can *you* become assessment literate—and quickly?

I believe you can do it simply by engaging in a one-night, two-night, or one-weekend reading of this book. Let me briefly lay out my game plan for the chapters to come. It represents my best sense of how to move from assessment *illiteracy* to assessment *literacy* in a heck of a hurry.

I've already asserted that assessment literacy hinges on an individual's understanding of the basic assessment concepts and procedures likely to have an impact on educational decisions. What I have not delved into is *who* decides *which* concepts and procedures ought to go into assessment literacy's "must be understood" backpack? The answer to this question hinges on *human judgment.*

It might surprise you to hear that the field of educational assessment, often assumed to be a tightly tied-down technical arena constrained by quantitative considerations and dependent on decimal points, is awash with human judgment. But it is. Indeed, the more one learns about educational assessment, the more one sees that judgment-based decisions surround us when we test students and use their responses to arrive at next-step educational actions.

In this book, the judgment you're relying on is mine. Over the 65 years I've been professionally engaged in education, my most serious career muck-ups have arisen from my asking educators to tackle too much at one time. Because of my frequent brushes with the adverse consequences of such excessive aspirations, I have become a staunch adherent of a *less-is-more* credo. So, even though the concepts and procedures related to educational assessment are myriad—potentially numbered in the hundreds—my less-is-more approach inclines me to select a small, readily internalizable set of educational assessment understandings to constitute the essence of assessment literacy. I have chosen six assessment-related concepts and procedures for you to understand and act upon.

These six anointed understandings were born from an even more authoritative source: the assessment-related guidelines in the most recent (2014) edition of the *Standards for Educational and Psychological Testing,* a joint publication of the three U.S. professional associations most concerned with educational assessment: the American Educational Research Association (AERA), the American Psychological Association (APA), and the National Council on Measurement in Education (NCME). The book is widely regarded as representing the best current thinking of leaders in the nation's educational measurement community. In fact, this volume (often called the *Joint Standards* because of its three collaborating sponsors) is usually referred to—and, more importantly, *deferred* to—in courtroom litigation involving educational tests. It also plays an influential role in the way tests are developed and evaluated. What's recommended in the *Joint Standards* is generally seen to represent "best educational assessment practices," and if commercial test firms do not follow its guidelines, those firms might find themselves in court defending their tests.

The *Joint Standards* is an enormously useful collection of assessment standards—"should do" and "shouldn't do" directives—for the promotion of assessment literacy. But it's also an *enormous collection*, period. Because the *Joint Standards* was developed by a prestigious committee of assessment luminaries who took over five years to complete their work, it is not surprising that the most recent revision of this document includes not only high-import aspects of educational assessment but also content that's of interest chiefly to assessment specialists.

The six assessment-related understandings you'll be encountering in this book represent my personal judgment about the most practical, action-influential concepts and procedures addressed in the *Joint Standards*. When you have internalized these six high-priority understandings, you will be *assessment literate* and well equipped to make the assessment-based educational decisions that you are likely to confront in your district, your school, or your classroom. That's not bad for a one-night, two-night, or one-weekend read!

A Final Introductory Heads-Up

Each of the next six chapters is organized around a single assessment-related understanding. Each begins with clarification of *why* the particular concept or procedure treated therein warrants an educator's thorough understanding. A colleague-to-colleague explanation, called "Understanding the Understanding," follows. In it, I'll delve into each understanding's component complexities.

Next, these chapters move on to a section called "The Understanding's Application," which presents a realistic scenario of a decision that would be best made by invoking the specific assessment-related understanding just featured. You'll have an opportunity to reach a personal decision regarding your own response to this exercise; then I'll provide my take on that same problem ("Jim's Decision"). Your decision in dealing with the exercise, of course, need not agree with mine; indeed, any differences between our judgments should be considered territory for further exploration. The goal here is to let you practice applying the assessment understanding. Again, the promotion of your *actionable* comprehension of these six understandings is this book's chief aim.

Chapters 2 through 7 all conclude with a section called "For the Truly Time-Pressed," which provides a bare-bones summary of the chapter's featured understanding. It's a ruthless compression of the content to its minimum essentials—a good set of reminders that's easy to refer to, discuss, and even share with colleagues, should you complete this book with an inclination to take part evangelistically in the promotion of assessment literacy.

The book's final chapter is a mite atypical for such wind-down chapters. It first provides you with a skinny synthesis of what went on in the preceding seven chapters. That, of course, is not so unusual. But it also presents you with a collection of four brief essays—a short stack of verbal kindling that you might employ to light an assessment-literacy bonfire under some of your coworkers. Accordingly, then, Chapter 8 is entitled "Wrapping Up, Reaching Out," because it is intended to supply you with a squished overview of the earlier seven chapters as well as one tangible way of personally spreading the word regarding educational assessment.

When you have finished reading the book, putting it aside with both reverence and sadness because there are no more chapters to read, you can employ two different sorts of "mental checks" to determine if your own level of comprehension is truly satisfactory:

- *Do you know when to use each of the book's assessment principles?* First, you'll need to estimate whether you are sufficiently comfortable in your mastery of every chapter's assessment-related understanding so that, if you were to be confronted with an educational decision, you'd know right away if it would help you make the impending decision. I call this check *influence judgment*. It's about using an understanding to influence an educational decision.
- *Can you explain these principles?* Second, you'll want to ask yourself if you understand each chapter's assessment-related understanding well enough to explain it to others. Do you grasp it well enough to supply a colleague with a reasonably clear explanation of the understanding, aloud, in writing, or via whatever mode of explanation—from PowerPoint presentation to puppet show—suits your audience? This check is about expanding the influence of your assessment

understanding and building assessment literacy where it is needed. It is needed everywhere.

Let's get started.

VALIDITY
The Overt in Search of the Covert

Validity is the most important concept in the world of educational testing. As the author of this book, and believing firmly in the merits of *all* its chapters, I can assure you that the one you're embarking on now stands alone atop this book's Most Important Chapter Mountain. I implore you to read it with extraordinary attentiveness.

Before I unfurl a sermon of support for validity's supreme importance, let me first invoke a bit of external confirmation from the superstar collection of assessment experts who revised the *Standards for Educational and Psychological Testing* (AERA, APA, & NCME, 2014). After first defining validity as "the degree to which evidence and theory support the interpretations of scores for proposed uses of tests," the *Joint Standards*—which is properly regarded as Holy Writ by most education assessment specialists—issues this verdict:

> Validity is, therefore, the most fundamental consideration in developing tests and evaluating tests. (p. 11).

I welcome the backup, of course, but it's the *therefore* component of this sentence that I invite you to pause over. It represents the understanding-based challenge of this chapter: to grasp not just what assessment validity is but also why it's so essential to test making and test interpreting. The conclusion I've drawn for myself, and the very conclusion I hope you will come to share, is that without validity, educational testing would have no point, no purpose, and no legitimate application. In this chapter, we will explore why.

Coping with the Covert

The reason we *teach* students is so that those students will *learn* stuff. This stuff to be learned, also known as "curricular aims," "educational goals," or "content standards," usually consists of *cognitive skills and bodies of knowledge*. Such skills and knowledge include mathematical or scientific facts and procedures, literacy and language skills, knowledge of civics, the ability to understand the past as well as apply history's lessons to the future and, basically, everything else we think of as "school stuff." Sometimes, educational goals include psychomotor skills, such as the large-muscle abilities sought in a physical education class or the small-muscle keyboarding capabilities promoted in a computer course. And some teachers also attempt to have their students acquire certain *affective* dispositions, such as a love of language, scientific curiosity, or an open and unbiased view of people.

Teachers and school administrators whose job it is to promote students' acquisition of skills, knowledge, and affect want to do that job well. They want their instructional efforts to be successful. And assessment is the tool that allows educators to figure out if students have mastered the curricular aims being sought. But here's where things get tricky.

The overwhelming majority of the time, teachers can't just *look* at a student and know whether the student has, in fact, learned what was taught. Someday, perhaps advances in brain-focused surgical and radiographic procedures will allow teachers to *actually see* the skills and knowledges caroming around inside a student's skull. For the foreseeable future, however, educators must rely on students' test-elicited *overt* evidence to come up with sufficiently accurate inferences about the *covert* nature of what students have or haven't learned.

As this chapter's title reminds us, educators use students' observable test responses to get a fix on those students' unobservable status. And this, dear reader, is why educational testing was born—and why it continues to exist. If tests can't do this job, they're a waste of everybody's time. Validity is the bedrock of our confidence in testing's ability to make the covert overt.

With that lead-in complete, it's now time for me to present the first and most important of this book's six must-master assessment understandings.

The Validity Understanding

Validity, the degree to which an evidence-based argument supports the accuracy of a test's interpretations for a proposed use of the test's results, is the necessary precursor to all educational assessment.

* * * * *

Understanding the Understanding

Because the aim of this book is to promote your personal mastery of six assessment-related understandings at a deep level, we need to dig into each understanding and isolate its most important elements. Accordingly, whenever a chapter's featured understanding is first rolled out for your consideration, you'll find it followed by a section like this one, set up to take apart, then clarify, its key features.

A closer look at the Validity Understanding reveals three interesting elements:

1. Validity depends on the quality of *an evidence-based argument*.
2. This argument is intended to support *the accuracy of a test's interpretations*.
3. This argument deals with the extent to which those interpretations *support the test's proposed use*.

We'll soon explore these three concepts one at a time. But first, a necessary *disavowal*: there is no such thing as a valid test. This simple statement is an essential repudiation of a prevalent misconception held by far too many educators. It's so important, I'll assert it again, with emphasis:

There is no such thing as a valid test.

Conversely, there is also no such thing as an *invalid test*.

As the Validity Understanding points out, validity isn't a quality of a test; it's a quality of the argument made *about* that test. The argument is built on evidence that the test will capture the kind of data it purports to capture and support the kinds of conclusions it is intended to support.

Further, because the process of determining validity is the process of evaluating an argument, it's necessarily reliant on good old human judgment. Are we persuaded by the evidence presented, or aren't we?

About now, you might reasonably be asking why I, an otherwise calm and collected author, seem to be getting into a tizzy about whether validity resides in a validity argument or in a test itself. Here is the trigger for my tizziness: once we decide that *a test itself* can be valid, we run the risk of believing the test is appropriate to use in all kinds of assessment situations. It's an awfully short trip from the erroneous "this is a *valid* test" to "this is *a* high-quality, *all-purpose test* that we can use to make every kind of covert status overt and guide every kind of assessment decision."

On the other hand, when we recognize that assessment validity arises from a human being's *judgment* about the strength of an argument, and that human judgment is not infallible, we are inclined to use caution both when selecting which tests to use and when evaluating the decision-relevant evidence they yield. Remember, those decisions affect our students' lives, often profoundly.

The two chief components of the assessment validity argument for all educational tests are depicted in Figure 2.1. An argument that fails to effectively address *both* interpretive accuracy *and* evidence of test-use support is a weak argument, worthy of rejection.

FIGURE 2.1 | Assessment Validity

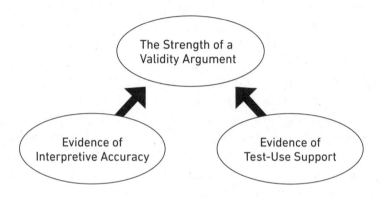

An Evidence-Based Argument

What are the so-called evidence-based arguments that are the heart of assessment validation?

Who makes these arguments? What do these arguments look like? Do they resemble some sort of formal disputation—a debate complete with time-limited presentations, rebuttals, and judge-rendered decisions? Or are these validity arguments like TV courtroom contests in which opposing attorneys call witnesses and muster evidence before deftly delivering summations to sway a teetering-either-way jury? Alas, it's decidedly less dramatic.

What typically happens in the generation of validity arguments is that the individuals who construct an educational test, while the test is being built, assemble validity, reliability, and item-quality information. When the test is released for use, a formal report containing this technical information is distributed to appropriate parties, such as a state's education authorities who authorized the test's development or, perhaps, local school district officials.

Generally, this technical report includes evidence dealing with the chief dimensions of the 2014 *Joint Standards*, including validity, reliability, and fairness. But the report's validity argument often looks nothing like the formal line of persuasive reasoning you'd get from an assistant DA on *Law & Order*. Instead, it's a simple presentation of evidence centered on the two assessment concerns we've named previously: (1) documentation attesting to the accuracy of score-based interpretations about test-takers' status and (2) documentation attesting to the extent to which those interpretations contribute to fulfillment of the test's intended purpose.

Typically, the more important the resulting test-linked decisions are, the more ample the technical documentation of the assessment's quality you can expect. For particularly high-stakes tests, the argument-supporting evidence can get intimidatingly complicated. Does this mean that all educators, you included, need to be comfortable digging into the viscera of an important test's technical report? Frankly, I don't think assessment literacy demands such sophisticated levels of measurement moxie from educators, and I'll try to defend that position later in this book.

What you'll be learning about in the remainder of this chapter are the basics of what's done when assessment validity is tackled. No, most educators, already short on discretionary time, don't need to study in detail what goes on in the collection and assembly of evidence underlying a validity argument. *But the validation process is not a mystery.* Teachers and administrators should not be intimidated if assessment whiz-bangs trot out these sorts of validity-related concepts and procedures. When you strip away the unfamiliar technical terminology, the actual steps taken when dealing with validity are quite straightforward.

Interpretive Accuracy

When we talk about test interpretation, what we're really talking about is the conclusions a test-user can draw about the test-taker's (covert) status, based on the results of that test.

When a student takes a test, what comes back is a score that's supposed to be indicative of the quality of the student's performance.

Sometimes it's a numerical score. Sometimes, it's a *percent correct*—the percentage of the test's items that the student answered correctly. Sometimes performance is reported in the form of a *raw score*—the number of points earned by a student with no attempt to convert this point total into a percentage of possible points. In still other instances, test-takers' performances are reported as *scale scores*. Scale scores are obtained by converting students' raw scores into a new statistically generated scale that's intended to reflect each test-taker's performance in a manner more suitable for subsequent statistical analysis. Because scale scores are becoming a prevalent way of reporting students' test performances, we'll look at them more closely in Chapter 5's treatment of score reporting.

Making sense of scores

No matter how students' performances are reported for a test, those who would use the test's results must decode what those scores mean. Yes, the test-user is required to make sense out of a score that, all by its lonesome, often makes no sense at all.

In the current edition of the *Joint Standards,* this sense making is referred to as an *interpretation.* Earlier editions described it as an *inference*—that is, a judgmentally derived conclusion about what a test score means. The two labels are interchangeable. Both describe someone's giving meaning to an otherwise tough-to-make-sense-of test score.

Especially for large-scale standardized tests, those who provide the test—measurement firms or state departments of education—will provide a score report that supplies guidance about how to arrive at a score-based interpretation of a test-taker's performance. Such guidelines often prove helpful to educators who must assign meaning to a student's test performance before acting on that meaning.

Identifying evidence of inference accuracy

This is the moment when educators need to consider the supporting evidence for the suggested inferences that the test developers have provided.

I've hinted that this evidence is not fingerprints, hair samples, or security camera footage. Let's cover what such evidence typically is:

- *Summarized sets of carefully collected item-quality judgments.* These judgments are made by item review panels of experienced teachers and academic content specialists. The more carefully that a test's items have been developed—and subsequently evaluated by appropriately oriented item-reviewers—the more confident we can be that the score-based interpretations suggested are accurate reflections of the caliber of a test-taker's performance.

- *Empirical studies dealing with the correctness of score-based inferences.* An example might be correlations computed between test-takers' scores and another indicator of those students' abilities, such as their teachers' independent judgments of the students' relative abilities made *prior* to a test's administration. A strong, positive correlation between these students' test scores and their teachers' judgments represents confirmatory evidence of the accuracy of the provided score-based interpretations.

That's often the evidence, and you'll usually find it in a test's technical report. But there is still a judgment to be made. Is this evidence strong enough, persuasive enough? Is it sufficient to convince would-be test-users that the score interpretation provided will be an accurate *overt* representation of the test-taker's *covert* status? Based on this evidence, it's up to the test-user to decide, "The test-based *interpretation* of student performance will be valid," or "The score-based *inference* about student skill mastery will be invalid." When we develop the habit of automatically thinking about *interpretation accuracy* rather than *test accuracy*, we position ourselves to make smarter test-based decisions.

Test-Use Supportiveness

To conclude this chapter's "Understanding the Understanding" section, we need to consider one final issue—that is, the degree to which an educational test elicits scores that do or do not support the purpose for which a test is to be used. Again, this is a conclusion to base on evidence rather than rhetoric (e.g., marketing copy from the test publisher). And, again, it's a conclusion that rests squarely on judgments about the quantity and strength of this evidence.

The test's intended use

In the abstract, it makes no sense to regard a test that's intended to accomplish Purpose X as automatically being suitable for accomplishing Purpose Z. If the Purpose X test is to be extended in attempting to accomplish Purpose *Z*, then evidence supporting its Purpose *Z* appropriateness should be provided. Our authoritative source agrees: the current version of the *Joint Standards* stresses the need to match a test's intended measurement mission with what the test can actually accomplish. And then there are the real-world consequences of mismatching test purpose and test capacity. As mentioned in Chapter 1, trying to use even a good educational test for an inappropriate purpose represents one of the most common, and most serious, mistakes made by educators whose assessment literacy is wanting.

The antidote is for those of us who are assessment literate to train ourselves to automatically raise a critical question early in the review of any already-developed educational test. This question, stripped to its plain-language essentials, is *"What is the intended use of this test?"* (For variety's sake, we might mix it up by asking, *"What decisions will be based on test-takers' scores?"*) Because assessment validity *requires* a test to support its intended use, it is crucial to get that intended use out on the table for all those involved to see.

The Validity Understanding also stresses that it's necessary to corral evidence regarding the match between a test's intended measurement use and what the test is actually measuring. Although the architects of the *Joint Standards* urge this action, they do not supply guidelines regarding satisfactory ways of going about it. Accordingly, the measurement community needs to come up with some defensible ways of showing that a test truly meshes with its measurement mission.

I have some suggestions. Panels of educators are often employed to review an under-development test's items—sometimes to ensure curricular alignment and sometimes to detect potentially biased items. Why not use the same panels to render systematically collected and analyzed judgments regarding the match between a test's intended measurement purpose (as identified, typically, by the test's developers) and the test itself? Using the test's score report, for example, and even a random selection of actual items, a panel of instructionally savvy educators could render individual judgments on a response form devised to establish the degree to which a test matches its intended purpose. Alternately, a group of panelists could individually review a test's items and score reports, then inductively come up with a written statement of what they believe to be the test's primary purpose. Those statements could subsequently be analyzed to discern how many panelists had accurately nailed the test's intended purpose.

Because the creators (or purchasers) of educational tests sometimes allege that their cherished test can do more than one thing, you'll frequently encounter a supposedly two-purpose or even three-purpose educational test. Well, for each supposed test use, the same assessment validation requirements are present. That is, if you're presented with a test purporting to serve Purposes X, Y, and Z, there should be evidence furnished to support both interpretive accuracy and the intended use for *each* of these ostensible purposes.

A test's possible purposes

With all this talk of purpose matching, perhaps we ought to backtrack a bit to isolate the various purposes a test might serve.

The three most common uses of educational tests, presented in Figure 2.2, are (1) to make comparisons among test-takers, (2) to improve ongoing instruction and learning, and (3) to evaluate instruction.

FIGURE 2.2 | The Three Primary Purposes of Educational Testing

Before we look briefly at each of these measurement functions, I want to state an unpleasant reality: *rarely* can an educational test perform more than one assessment function satisfactorily. More often than not, we deceive ourselves when we pretend that tests can hit two bull's-eyes with a single arrow. With few exceptions, multimission educational assessments of sufficient quality simply do not exist. Let's see why this is so.

Testing for comparison. Comparison-focused testing has been around since testing first toddled onto the scene. When we test for comparisons among test-takers, we distinguish standards-masterers from the yet-to-masterers, the most capable from the least capable, the *A* students from the *B* students, and the likely to succeed in college from those less likely to do so. Because comparison-focused testing typically leads to more enlightened decisions about individual test-takers, it is not surprising that testing for comparison has been a prominent purpose of educational testing for as long as educational testing has existed.

Historically, the most prominent use of standardized tests in the United States has been to compare the relative ability of test-takers. It all started during World War I with a test called the "Army Alpha," administered to nearly two million Army recruits to see which of those men were most likely to succeed in the Army's officer training programs. It presented recruits with a series of verbal and quantitative problems consistent with the Army Alpha's avowed measurement task—namely, to spread out examinees' performance so that the most intellectually able of those recruits could be assigned to the Army's officer training facilities.

This new test worked remarkably well, yielding highly useful comparative information so that a given recruit could be identified as falling in, for example, the 91st percentile, the 82nd percentile, or the 45th percentile in relation to a normative group of recruits who had previously completed the Army Alpha. Because of its widely acknowledged success in carrying out this comparative mission, the test development and test evaluation procedures utilized with this World War I examination have dominated American educational testing for more than 100 years. Over this century-long span, the comparative testing procedures derived from the Army Alpha have often been misapplied for other-than-comparative assessment purposes. Without question, there is a role for comparative measurement in educational testing. Problems arise, however, when a comparatively oriented test is employed for other-than-comparative purposes.

Testing to improve ongoing instruction and learning. A second prominent purpose of educational testing, not surprisingly, has been to better educate students. If tests supply evidence of students' current knowledge or skills—and provide it in a timely manner, so that action can be taken to improve mastery of such knowledge and skills—then teachers can use this assessment-elicited evidence to revise their instructional activities for the better. Moreover, students can also employ such evidence to help them revamp the way that they are trying to learn things.

A key to capitalizing on a test destined for a learning-improvement mission is to make sure the test yields results in a way that teachers and students can readily incorporate a results-based inference into a next-step instructional activity. One of the key considerations in doing so is to make sure students' performances are reported at a "grain size" that can be readily translated into subsequent actions. If results are reported too broadly, they are hard to synthesize and act on. If results are reported in too-tiny chunks, it is difficult to make coalesced and actionable sense out of them. Yes, building a test so it yields results at a suitable grain size is crucial to the improvement of instruction and learning.

Testing to evaluate instruction. The third major purpose of educational testing is to gather data that will help determine the quality of one or more already-completed instructional activities. Such a mission might be to evaluate the instruction provided by an individual teacher or by a group of teachers throughout an entire school or district, and the question it seeks to answer is "How good was the instruction provided?" The answer might be followed by inquiry into how to improve ineffective instruction or how to get other educators to emulate the instructional tactics of demonstrably effective teaching.

For better and for worse, testing's evaluation function is very familiar to educators working in today's "era of accountability." We can trace the widespread use of accountability in the United States to the 1965 Elementary and Secondary Education Act (ESEA), federal legislation including the requirement that school performance and progress toward academic goals be tracked in order to help ensure the quality of public schools. That was, and still is, a worthy goal. It's a defensible application of educational testing, but only if the right tests are employed for the job.

How a test's purpose factors into evaluation of validity

Just as there is a need to identify evidence supporting the accuracy of test-based interpretations about students, there is a similar *purpose-focused* evidentiary need. Anyone creating a test for *any* of the purposes outlined—comparison, instruction, or evaluation—must provide evidence that the test is appropriate for the chosen purpose.

When the purpose is comparison. If an educational test is employed for comparative purposes, it is important to supply evidence that the test can consistently differentiate among test-takers on a variable (such as academic aptitude) deemed necessary for accomplishing the test's purpose. Beyond such evidence, however, there's also a need for evidence attesting to the accuracy of the comparisons being made. If, for instance, an interim test is being used in a middle school to predict which students are likely to flop on the state's 10th grade accountability test, evidence should be assembled to indicate that the resultant test-based predictions are accurate.

When the purpose is instruction. If test is to be used for instructional purposes, we need evidence that the test will yield results that are *actionable* and, ideally, are *readily* actionable. For example, if we were ginning up a new classroom test that a district's science teachers could use to prepare students for taking high school science courses, we'd certainly want to get teachers' reactions to the new test. Do they see the results it reports as being truly useful for informing their next-step instructional decisions? We might also be persuaded by evidence indicating that teachers who have used the test's results to inform instruction reported that the test-informed decisions made a positive impact on students' learning.

What we often see these days are so-called instructionally helpful educational tests developed by using the procedures borrowed from the creators of comparatively purposed tests. Such wrong-purposed tests typically yield unclear amalgams of evidence, little of which can be acted on to arrive at sound instructional decisions.

When the purpose is evaluation. With a test created to serve an evaluative function, such as a high-stakes achievement test, purpose-focused evidence must demonstrate the test is *instructionally sensitive*. This means the test is capable of distinguishing between well-taught and badly taught students. High scores on the test reflect successful instruction; low scores reflect the opposite. An example of the sort of evidence needed to signify a test's instructional sensitivity could be data demonstrating that students who were taught what the test measured routinely generated scores higher than those generated by students who weren't taught the measured content. (I know this sounds obvious, yet many so-called achievement tests actually measure students' *inherited* or *affluence-related* smarts rather than what they have been taught. Evidence of instructional sensitivity might indicate, at least, that a test could differentiate between taught and untaught students.) If no instructional-sensitivity evidence is presented, this means a necessary attribute of assessment validity is missing, and it's fundamentally inappropriate to use such a test to evaluate educational quality.

Annoyingly, there's no button to press on a computer that will unerringly signify whether a validity argument is sufficiently strong to justify an educational test's use for a given educational purpose. At least one human being, usually more, needs to review the persuasiveness of an argument and the quality of its assembled evidence, then judge whether a specific test is good enough to warrant its use. Assessment validity, as you can see, is a judgmental enterprise.

The Understanding's Application

Hopefully, you are now feeling sufficiently comfortable with the Validity Understanding (still happily nestled on page 18) so that you can apply it in a hypothetical scenario I'm about to provide. After you have arrived at your response to the exercise—mentally, in writing, or spelled out in nautical semaphore—you might care to look at my own response to the same exercise, presented on page 32. On the other hand, you might prefer not to look. Your book, your choice.

Imagine that you are an experienced social studies teacher who has recently been appointed assistant principal of a large urban high school. During your first few months in this new administrative post, you have been asked to become a member of a district advisory committee whose mission is to advise the school board on the selection of high school accountability tests in English language arts (ELA) and mathematics. Students' scores on these two tests, administered once a year in the spring, will be used as prominent factors in evaluating the instructional effectiveness of the district's high schools. In your state, school districts have a statutorily declared option to employ (1) the state's annually administered accountability tests, (2) commercial achievement tests of comparable quality, or (3) district-developed tests demonstrably of equal rigor to the state-administered tests.

For the past several weeks, you have been chairing a subcommittee charged with deciding whether to recommend the adoption of a pair of commercially developed achievement tests for grade 11. Your sub-committee has been gravitating toward selecting these commercially developed tests because of doubts that the district has the assessment expertise to develop ELA and math tests that would be "of equal rigor" to the state's tests. Moreover, because many district educators have expressed substantial dissatisfaction with the state-developed test option, your subcommittee's decision regarding the commercial test is likely to be influential in guiding the district advisory committee's test-selection recommendation.

The test you are evaluating is known as the Three Letter Test (TLT), a label apparently chosen because of the popularity of the SAT and ACT for use as college admissions examinations. Developmental work on the TLT has taken about three years, and evidence of its quality is available in a TLT technical manual that your subcommittee has found to be quite clear. Evidence is presented regarding both the mathematics test and the ELA test.

Because the TLT is deliberately intended to serve as a competitor to the SAT and ACT, its technical manual provides substantial documentation of the degree to which secondary students' scores on the TLT are as predictive of high school students' subsequent college grades as are the SAT and ACT. The SAT versus TLT correlation is .73—quite strong. The ACT versus TLT correlation is .78—slightly stronger.

In addition, because the SAT and ACT provide detailed descriptions of their content coverage, the architects of the TLT were quite explicit in laying out the nature of the skills and knowledge measured by their test's items. Moreover, your subcommittee's analysis of the skills and knowledge being tested by the two TLT tests indicates that the content of the two tests is remarkably similar to the content identified in your district's official curriculum.

Finally, because a particularly rigorous process was employed to detect and eliminate any under-development TLT items that seemed to contain assessment bias, the TLT technical manual contains a thoroughgoing description of those bias-detection procedures and the number of items excised from the test because of their potential assessment bias.

Although most members of your subcommittee believe the content of the TLT matches the curricular targets emphasized instructionally by your district's educators, they worry that the adoption of the commercially created TLT will cost the district approximately 30 percent more than would the use of state-administered tests.

Given this admittedly meager context, if you and your subcommittee mates were attempting to apply the Validity Understanding in arriving at a decision regarding adoption of the TLT, what would that recommendation be?

....

JIM'S DECISION

If I were a member of your subcommittee, after fawning briefly over your skilled subcommittee leadership, I'd come down strongly against recommending the TLT to the school board. Because I support, almost obsequiously, the Joint Standards' *notion that assessment validity is the most fundamental construct in educational assessment, in settings such as this fictitious one, I find myself searching immediately for evidence of score interpretation accuracy and, thereafter, for evidence that a test's score-based interpretations support the intended use of the test. Although other considerations are important, and factors such as bias elimination and the price of a test can play a prominent role in a decision on whether to use a given test, validity evidence trumps everything else for me. And in this exercise, my judgment tells me that assessment validity is not present, because there's insufficient evidence that the two TLT tests will do a satisfactory job of accomplishing the tests' intended use.*

The needed measurement function in this instance was an evaluative one: the chosen tests needed to do a reasonable job in evaluating the instructional success of district schools. But there was no evidence—none at all—presented to indicate the TLT tests are capable of doing this. The correlations between the TLT and the two nationally recognized college entrance exams (the SAT and ACT) are not necessarily indicative of the TLT's evaluative strength; they are merely reflective of the two tests' predictive strength in a comparative context. Were we considering the SAT or ACT, I'd probably be making the same negative recommendation.

....

For the Truly Time-Pressed

It's time to wrap up our treatment of the most significant understanding you'll be encountering in this book. Let's look one last time at the chapter's featured understanding, then remind ourselves—ever so suc-cinctly—of its most important elements:

The Validity Understanding

Validity, the degree to which an evidence-based argument supports the accuracy of a test's interpretations for a proposed use of the test's results, is the necessary precursor to all educational assessment.

* * * * *

When you think about assessment validity, several things should come instantly to mind.

1. The degree of assessment validity hinges on the quality of an evidence-based argument, and validity most definitely does not reside in any individual test.
2. There must be evidence indicating the degree to which score-based interpretations about students' unobservable status will be accurate.
3. Additional evidence should be available to demonstrate that results of the test will meaningfully support the test's purpose.

In short, assessment validity represents the quality of an evidence-based argument attesting to *the accuracy of score-based inferences about test-takers* and *the test's utility in supporting the test's intended use.* Finally, the quality of this validity argument is determined not by pre-determined numerical requirements but by good old human judgment.

In a very explicit fashion, if an educational test washes out on assessment validity, there's really no need to consider further the test's strengths or its weaknesses. Unlike baseball, where it takes three strikes to get a batter out, educational testing is a one-strike contest. If the test loses out on validity, it's not just out—the whole game is over.

3 RELIABILITY
Assessment's Righteous Rascal

Reliability is a consummately good thing. We want it from our automobiles, our cell phones, and our best friends. We *can count on* things that are reliable; we can trust them, and they won't let us down. In contrast, *unreliability* sucks. It was always thus.

Given reliability's righteousness, it's not surprising that educators want the tests they use to be reliable. Even folks who have never had formal assessment training know that when a test is being evaluated for quality, the test's reliability is almost certain to be involved. Some even know that reliability is usually reported as a correlation coefficient, and that strong positive reliability coefficients of, say, .80 or .90 are considered good, while lower coefficients of .50 or .60 are considered less good. Although there certainly are educators who know what it means to talk about a test's reliability, far more *only sort of know* ... and that sort-of-knowing has consequences. The assessment understanding presented in this chapter will put everyone who's currently in the sort-of-know category on a more informed path.

Be warned: this path is not without its twists! As we will explore in the pages to come, there are three different ways to determine a given test's reliability. Moreover, figuring out which way is the *right* way can be very tricky. For all of reliability's great reputation, it's a real rascal—hard to pin down.

In this chapter, we'll be looking at the three distinctive incarnations of reliability evidence, examining how they are born and how they can be evaluated for their worthiness. Most important, we'll focus on how *un*interchangeable the three sorts of reliability evidence are and why knowing which type of evidence to examine in which circumstances allows us to select tests that will support better educational decision making. After we get straight on which category of reliability evidence is appropriate for a given test's intended use, the next step is to decide if this "right-category" evidence of reliability is, in fact, sufficiently convincing to warrant our use of the test. As with assessment validity, this decision boils down to judgment.

Reliability: Consistency of the Right Sort

Synonyms can sometimes help us understand the nuances of similar or equivalent terms. Fortunately, there is a particularly suitable synonym, waiting on the bench and ready to be sent in as a suitable substitute for *assessment reliability*. This synonym is *consistency*. The degree to which a test is reliable is the degree to which that test measures with consistency. And the specific evidence of consistency employed when making a case for a test's reliability must mesh with the use to which test-takers' scores will be put. In other words, form must follow function. If a test is planned to serve a particular measurement function—be it comparative, instructional, or evaluative—then the evidence of the test's reliability must support that specific use.

Must-Master Equivalencies

The two equations in Figure 3.1 capture significant truths regarding the reliability of educational tests. The first equation defines the essence of assessment reliability, and it's simple enough to commit to memory. The second equation might not seem too complicated a concept, but the alarming infrequency with which we encounter educational tests whose reliability evidence matches their intended uses suggests it's more of challenge than you might think.

Here's how it usually goes. Someone—or some group—touts the wonders of a new educational test, perhaps for instructional improvement or for educational evaluation. At the same time, those touters supply reliability evidence for the test. Because so few educators understand the triple-headed nature of reliability evidence, the suitability of the presented reliability evidence is rarely questioned. And so, the touted test is selected, even when its consistency was ascertained using the wrong reliability evidence. Consequently, we often put our faith in a test and trust it to do a job for which it's not actually designed. What our schools need are assessment-literate educators capable of distinguishing between supportive and irrelevant reliability evidence and sufficiently courageous to call foul when irrelevant evidence is offered.

FIGURE 3.1 | Key Reliability Equivalencies

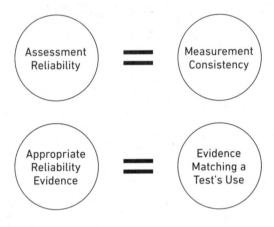

Reliability Resides in a Test

You will recall from your attentive reading of Chapter 2 that assessment validity refers not to the qualities of a test itself but to the accuracy of a test-based *inference* about a test-taker's covert cognitive status. Educators make inferences (or interpretations) about a student's knowledge or skills based on that student's test scores.

However, when it comes to reliability, the attribution game changes dramatically. Unlike validity, assessment reliability resides not in a test-based inference *but in the test itself*. Accordingly, educators should expect that the tests they use will be accompanied by evidence regarding reliability. Not surprisingly, the more important that a test's intended use is, the more reliability evidence should accompany the test. Whereas a teacher might not go bonkers about the absence of reliability evidence for a brief classroom quiz covering content taught in a single class session, the absence of reliability evidence for a significant diploma-denial test would be almost unthinkable.

Although educators themselves can assemble reliability evidence for tests, and sometimes do so, more often we'll find busy educators weighing the worth of the reliability evidence presented by those who have built or evaluated a particular test. These educators might be classroom teachers who are deciding whether to employ a set of commercially published classroom tests or educational administrators who are deciding whether to advocate adoption of a test to be used in evaluating teachers' instructional effectiveness.

Arriving at a decision regarding whether a given educational test's reliability is good enough to warrant the test's use is a two-step process. First, an appropriate variety of reliability evidence must be scrutinized—evidence that's clearly suitable for the test's intended use. Second, a judgment must be made regarding the degree to which the chosen reliability evidence is strong enough so that the test's users can be sufficiently confident of the test's assessment consistency.

This sort of two-step reliability dance is much easier to describe than it is to implement, and here's why. First, over the years, test development groups have gotten used to collecting certain kinds of reliability evidence and presenting it as a suitable way of determining a test's reliability. For instance, commercial developers of large-scale standardized tests almost always promote their tests' yumminess by wheeling out reliability coefficients reflecting high levels of test consistency—a test-reliability coefficient of, say, .90 or .96—based on how similarly the test's items are measuring what the test measures. (The closer to 1.0 that these reliability coefficients are, the more assurance a potential test-user is supposed to possess.) Anyone who questions traditionally acceptable evidence is apt to be regarded as an infidel, either out of step with the way reliability has always been traditionally determined or just mildly deranged.

Second, even with an assembly of appropriate reliability evidence, determining whether such evidence of consistency is sufficiently compelling to warrant the test's use is no picnic. There's no electronic device to make the job quick and easy, and no set of sacred criteria to invoke. Because of the distinctiveness of the settings in which reliability evidence is gathered, there's simply no one-size-fits-all set of guidelines to tell us what constitutes sufficiently persuasive reliability evidence.

That leads us to this chapter's featured assessment-related under-standing. Please give it a slow, thought-drenched read. Then read it once again for good measure. It's important.

The Reliability Understanding

Assessment reliability, the consistency with which a test measures whatever it measures, is represented by three conceptually different kinds of evidence, and it should be reported for both test-taker groups and individual test-takers.

* * * * *

Understanding the Understanding

We'll do in this chapter what we did in the last: look carefully at the assessment understanding and analyze its chief components.

In the Reliability Understanding, you'll see three important features:

1. Reliability is defined as the consistency with which a test measures what it measures.
2. There are three fundamentally different sorts of evidence that can be used to indicate a test's reliability.
3. It's necessary to report reliability evidence for individual test-takers as well as for groups of test-takers.

Time to dig into each of these.

In Praise of Consistency

There was probably a moment, way back in time and probably undoc-umented, when a handful of folks were just beginning to create large-scale educational tests and just starting to think about how those tests might be used. Surely, they concluded that if test results were going to be the basis for making educational decisions, the test being used ought to yield results that were regular rather than erratic.

For instance, these early architects of large-scale testing might have thought, if a teacher gives the same test to the same student twice, the teacher wants to know that the student will achieve basically the same score both times (providing there was no additional studying or looking up of answers between the two test sessions). Or, if teachers use slightly different versions of a test to keep first-period takers from revealing its secrets to third-period takers, those teachers want to be confident that both forms will measure with the same degree of accuracy. Finally, teachers want to know that the items on a test are all measuring what's to be measured without introducing irrelevant or unrelated content. Teachers want these things so they can trust that a test will generate good data—data serving as the basis for appropriate educational decisions.

One of the reasons that a reliable test is patently superior to an unreliable test is because test reliability is a necessary precursor to test validity. Think of it this way: it's impossible to conclude that a test score will support an accurate inference about a students' covert skill status unless we are first convinced that the test is measuring what it measures with sufficient consistency. Yes, our top two assessment understandings have an important relationship, but like many relationships, it's complicated. I can sum it up like this:

For validity to be present, a test must be reliable, but a reliable test may or may not yield valid interpretations.

In other words, we may have a test that provides excellent evidence of reliability, but our determination that a test is reliable is not enough to convince us that our test-based inferences about its results are valid. Reliability is a necessary condition for valid test-based interpretations. But, on its own, it's not a sufficient one. It's part of the evidence for determining validity, but only one part.

Three Consistency Requirements, Three Kinds of Evidence

Consider the 12-inch wooden ruler. It's a familiar presence in elementary school classrooms, where it's used to measure the length of all kinds of objects. Now consider that a century or so ago, teachers commonly used the 12-inch wooden ruler to dole out corporal punishment to misbehaving students. This is a simple example of how the same tool can be used for very different purposes. And, clearly, evaluating the success of a ruler as a measurement tool and evaluating its success as a hand-whacking tool would call for different sorts of evidence.

An educational test is another tool that can be employed in different ways—three different ways, to be exact. Each way requires a conceptually related but decisively different sort of reliability evidence. These three varieties are presented together in Figure 3.2.

FIGURE 3.2 | Reliability Evidence in Three Varieties

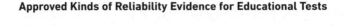

Approved Kinds of Reliability Evidence for Educational Tests

Test-Retest Reliability Evidence

Alternative Form Reliability Evidence

Internal Consistency Reliability Evidence

Test-retest reliability evidence

In the routine course of trying to educate students, teachers encounter situations where some students must complete a test at a time other than the time when most students take it. There are a host of reasons why a student might miss a test and have to make it up a few hours, days, or even weeks later: illness or injury, family obligations, extracurricular opportunities, and so on.

In such situations, the teachers who are administering the test need the instrument they are using to do its assessment job the same way *over time*. If the delay between two time-separated tests does not seem to be interminably long, and students taking the makeup test have not been influenced by any intervening events, instructional or otherwise, since the test was administered to the rest of the class, there should be stability between the score a student would have achieved on Test Occasion 1 and the score that the same student would have achieved on Test Occasion 2. In earlier versions of the *Joint Standards,* this form of over-time reliability evidence was referred to as *stability evidence of reliability.* Many psychometricians still use this label ("stability") to describe such evidence. The current edition of the *Joint Standards* (AERA, APA, & NCME, 2014), however, now refers to this as *test-retest reliability evidence.*

All kinds of factors, often not readily isolatable, could contribute to a test's lack of stability. To illustrate, perhaps certain of the test's items are phrased ambiguously so that, if some students are asked to respond to an item twice, those students would arrive at different interpretations of what the item actually means. Then, too, there might be something going on in a test-taker's private life that would incline the student to regard a test item's content in a meaningfully different manner. When we educators look at the estimates of a test's reliability, we need not try to isolate the specific causes of inconsistency; it's enough to review consistency in a more general manner. If a test appears to be less than reliable, we can and should walk away and leave it to the test's developers to figure out how to enhance that test's consistency.

One common way that test developers collect test-retest reliability evidence is to administer a test, then re-administer that same test to the same students after some time has elapsed. Test-takers' scores from the two testing occasions are then correlated; the resultant correlation coefficient is thereafter referred to at the test's "reliability coefficient." Usually, a test-maker will identify the particular nature of the reliability coefficient that's being presented along with an educational test, but not always. In fact, one of the most serious shortcomings in the way today's educators cite evidence of assessment reliability is by referring to the three different sorts of reliability evidence as though they were essentially interchangeable. They are not.

Given the care with which many nationally standardized tests are developed, it is not unusual to encounter strong, positive test-retest correlation coefficients in the low .90s. With less carefully created tests, such as district-developed achievement exams or a teacher's own classroom assessments, test-retest reliability coefficients are typically somewhat lower, say, .80 to .90.

A quick digression for anyone who is unfamiliar with the meaning of correlation coefficients: if a group of students completed two administrations of the same test a month apart, and every student's score was *precisely* the same on both testing occasions, the resultant correlation coefficient between the two sets of results would be a positive 1.0. Yet, if there were small differences between the two sets of scores—perhaps for only a handful of students—then the correlation coefficient might drop to, say, .92. If the scores were somewhat similar, but many students earned seriously different scores, then the coefficient might be, say, .66. If the two sets of scores were all over the lot, with no consistency whatsoever on the two testing occasions, the resulting correlation coefficient would be close to zero.

Alternate-form reliability evidence

A complicating factor with makeup tests is the risk that the later test-takers will seek to discover what was on the test before their makeup test date, then double down on studying what they heard was being assessed on the test's items. To minimize any contamination that might arise when earlier test-takers discuss what was tested with later test-takers, test developers frequently create multiple forms of the same test—different versions that are intentionally equivalent. They do this by juggling items and making certain that whatever content is being measured by the different forms has been assessed in a comparable fashion. Test developers can usually come up with reasonable alternate forms of a test—alternate forms reflecting equal difficulty and content challenges for students. At least the architects of standardized educational tests make a good faith effort to do so.

To calculate the *alternate-form reliability* of a test, all we need do is to administer two different test forms to the same students, then compare their two separate sets of performances via computation of a traditional correlation coefficient between the two separate sets of test scores.

As with all correlation coefficients that are employed to represent a test's measurement consistency, the more developmental care that has been given to the generation of the test forms involved, the more likely there will be a strong, positive correlation between students' performances on the two test forms. A carefully constructed test will come back around .90 and a less carefully crafted one near .70 or so.

Given that an increasing number of educational tests these days are being administered as computer-generated tests, the need for intact, unmodifiable alternate test forms is declining. This is because computer programs can, via an instantaneous internal digital dance of some mystical sort, provide equivalently challenging tests for individual students.

Such software-sired alternate forms, of course, must follow a digital item-selection process that ensures, insofar as possible, the equivalence of different computer-generated forms. Even so, test developers must still provide evidence of the consistency with which computer-generated tests measure what they are purported to measure.

Internal consistency reliability evidence

The final entrant in the reliability-evidence sweepstakes happens to be the most frequently presented form of reliability evidence. This is due, in no small part, to the relative ease with which it is calculated. Whereas the calculation of test-retest reliably evidence and alternate-form reliability evidence both require two test administrations, the generation of *internal consistency reliability evidence* needs only a single administration.

Although it's a simpler form of consistency to calculate, internal consistency reliability evidence is more difficult to explain. What's at stake is the *homogeneity of a test's items.* In other words, it focuses on the degree to which a test's items are doing the same sort of measurement job throughout the test—that is, measuring the same skills or knowledge in the same way. If the items are doing this well, the resultant internal consistency reliability coefficient will be high. If, however, a test's items are measuring connected but distinguishable things, such as three related but separate mathematical skill sets focused on geometry, algebra, and measurement, then a test's internal consistency coefficient will be lower.

Sometimes educators *want* to measure a broad, general amalgam of related skills and knowledge, and the kind of test used to do this might be described as an assessment of overall "quantitative mastery." But at other times, particularly when the goal is to improve instruction, educators want to measure *more instructionally targeted* sets of skills and knowledge. For those two importantly different measurement missions, we would hope for meaningfully *different* sorts of internal consistency reliability coefficients—higher in the first case, where the aim is to gather data on lots of skills and knowledge, and lower in the second, when we want a sharper focus on fewer sets of skills of knowledge. Let me underscore this point: unlike the other two categories of reliability evidence, internal consistency reliability evidence needs to be approached with the understanding that a higher reliability coefficient is *not* an automatic winner. When evaluating the quality of internal consistency coefficients, different expectations come into play depending on *the purpose for which a test is being used.*

Suppose, for example, that a state department of education wishes to use students' scores on an annual accountability test to rank the overall quality of the state's school districts and, beyond this purpose, to rank the success of the schools within those districts. Two end-of-year achievement tests are administered each spring, one in ELA and one in mathematics. Again, the purpose of this accountability test is *comparison.* Beyond distributing the annual ranking reports, the educators within these districts receive no data that might be applied for instructional purposes, such as diagnostic subscale scores for separate ELA and mathematics skills. Indeed, local districts and schools are urged to devise their own instructional improvement strategies to best match the distinctive student bodies and the strengths of their unique teaching staffs.

Now suppose that a neighboring state has focused annual testing program on *instructional improvement*. Its mandated ELA and mathematics tests are also administered every spring, but with the clear intent that districts and schools examine each year's results to improve the design of instructional activities for the coming school year. Because the tests' results are presented as diagnostic subscale scores for separate, instructionally "assailable" ELA and mathematics skills, over summer vacation educators are to use the tests' results to devise "new and improved" instructional procedures for next year.

Here's a one-question, two-part puzzle for you to ponder: In which of the two states should state officials be *happy* with strong internal consistency reliability coefficients (.90 or higher) for their state tests, and in which of the two states should state officials be *unhappy* with the same high internal consistency reliability coefficients? Take a moment to ruminate before answering.

That's right—the first state needs tests with high internal consistency reliability coefficients, and the second state needs tests with lower ones. To put it more emphatically, only if a large-scale accountability test is to be used for comparative purposes—*with little or no instructional dividends promised*—should educators be swayed to select it because of high internal consistency reliability coefficients. This is because the test is promising to supply only an overall picture of scores for schools and districts, not reports that provide the diagnostic data necessary to serve instructionally supportive purposes. For a state using a comparison-focused accountability test, an internal consistency reliability coefficient of, say, .92, would be terrific.

In the state where the annual accountability test is intended to provide instructionally relevant information for enhancing next year's teaching, it would *not be* wonderful to have one enormously homogeneous collection of fundamentally similar broad-mission items. These teachers need information regarding their instructional successes and failures in the promotion of *separate* ELA and math skills and bodies of knowledge measured at instructionally addressable size. Accordingly, an internal consistency reliability coefficient of .70 or so might be just right, indicative that a test's distinctive subsets of items might be doing their separate jobs. A high internal consistency estimate, in contrast, would indicate that a tradition-anointed quest for overall item homogeneity had once again trumped instructional good sense. When the decision makers haven't grasped this aspect of assessment literacy, they might choose the "more reliable" test, and ask teachers to use it to improve instruction, even though the results it provides have scant utility for that purpose.

As this short exercise has underscored, as with test-retest evidence and alternate-form evidence, conclusions about the suitability of internal consistency evidence are reached via human judgment. All these judgments are typically based on the sizes of the reliability coefficients— but always against a backdrop of intended test usage.

Deciding how strong a set of reliability evidence must be before it is thought to be "strong enough" represents a rough challenge. In general, the more experience that someone has in dealing with diverse sorts of reliability evidence, the more confidently that such a person can say, "This is strong evidence of the test's reliability, and it's a suitable sort of reliability evidence for the sort of test we have in mind." If you do not personally possess such experience, *and very few educators do*, then one option would be to enlist the experience-abetted advice of a colleague who has already spent time in the trenches doing serious battle with such reliability indicators. I have one other sort of solution strategy that I'll offer for your consideration in Chapter 8. Yes, you can regard the previous sentence as an undisguised "tease" aimed at getting you to keep reading.

Let's turn now to some underexamined aspects of reliability.

Assessment Consistency for Groups and for Solo Students

When most educators think about a test's reliability, they usually focus on whatever reliability coefficients are reported as a reflection of the test's measurement consistency. As noted, higher, positive coefficients are generally seen as winners (evidence for using a test), and lower, less positive coefficients are usually thought to be nonwinners (evidence for not using it).

Classification-consistency indices

In addition to the more conventional reporting of correlation coefficients focused on reliability, it is becoming increasingly common for test-makers to make available estimates of *classification consistency*. When such evidence is featured in descriptions of a test's technical quality, what's reported is not the similarity of test-takers' specific scores but, rather, the percent of identical test-taker classifications based on those scores. In other words, the report would not cite the percent of students who achieved the same scores on two different forms of the test, but the percentage of students whose scores on two different forms of the test fell into the same classification category both times (e.g., two *Advanced*s, nine *Proficient*s, and so on). Classification categories often determine decisions made about test-takers, so sometimes this approach to reliability is referred to as a *decision-consistency* system. Many educators prefer such indicators of classification consistency over conventional reliability coefficients because the classification-consistency estimates are more intuitively understandable and decidedly less opaque than most statistically conjured reliability indices.

The standard error of measurement

Whereas group-focused estimates such as reliability coefficients or classification-consistency estimates can be immensely helpful in judging the worthiness of an educational test, there are many occasions when we need assessment-consistency evidence regarding an individual student. For instance, having access to reliability evidence would be useful when making decisions about whether to place a low-performing student in an intensive (and costly) remediation program or whether to assign an honorary achievement award to a high-performing student.

To deal with this need, assessment-literate educators typically rely on the *standard error of measurement* (SEM). An SEM functions in much the same way that the error margins used in pre-election polling do. These survey reports might state, for example, that Candidate A is preferred by 45 percent of the voters, while Candidate B is preferred by 39 percent of the voters—*but that there is "a plus-or-minus error margin of three percentage points."* This error margin indicates that if the sampling survey were to be repeated, odds are the results would come out the same way within the specified plus-or-minus error margin. In the educational testing arena, SEMs work the same way for those interpreting an individual student's test scores. For example, if students' test scores were being reported on a scale of 200 to 400 points, and a student had received a scale score of 245, an SEM of ±3 points would indicate that if the student retook the test, the student would probably score between

242 and 248 a specified percent of the time. (This "specified percent of time," based on normal-curve probabilities for plus or minus one SEM, turns out to be about 67 percent. It is also possible to calculate error margins of ±2 SEMs which, of course, would result in an even wider error margin of about 95 percent.)

SEMs are calculated according to (1) the statistical spread of test-takers' scores on an exam along with (2) the reliability coefficient that has been calculated for the exam. The greater the spread of students' scores, the larger the SEM will be. Similarly, the lower the reliability of a test, the larger the SEM will be.

SEMs are quite easy to compute and, as you can see, they're a useful check on putting too much faith in a test's measurement precision. After all, in most instances of students' retaking an exam that they'd taken an hour earlier, few students would achieve the exact same score both times. In short, the SEM is a way of bringing the real world and its host of extraneous factors, such as failures of concentration, carelessness, and so on, into the evaluation of calculated reliability for a test.

It's important to remember that the educators considering the use of a particular test often have an array of *different* reliability coefficients to consider. The reliability coefficient selected to calculate the SEM for any given test should be consonant with the intended use of the test involved. For instance, if you were interested in an SEM for a situation in which a test-retest reliability application was being employed, then it would be *inappropriate* for the SEM calculation formula to employ an internal consistency reliability coefficient. Unfortunately, educators do this sort of thing all the time. They may possess a general idea about the role of an SEM, but they don't realize that a test's developers have been cavalier in determining how to calculate the specific SEM being reported.

The Understanding's Application

Please assume for the next few paragraphs that you're a member of a middle school's Assessment Tools Committee. The committee's chief task is to review any commercially available or district-developed assessments that might be used in your middle school. You can assume that you are a teacher or an administrator in your school, because this is a malleable application exercise in which you have considerable say about such make-believe assumptions.

The current charge to the committee stems from your school district's recent development of sets of middle school interim tests in (1) mathematics, (2) English language arts, and (3) science. A task force has created four interim tests, for use in grades 7 or 8, in each of those three subject areas. Teachers are to decide for their individual classes whether the interim tests should be used at 7th grade, 8th grade, or at both grades. The tests would be used every two or three months to help teachers identify students' subject-matter strengths and weaknesses. The rationale behind the move is that teachers who can detect students' skill-related weaknesses can go on to devise instructional activities to address those weaknesses; by doing so, they will be able to advance students' mastery of specific curricular aims over the course of the school year. Each of the four 50-minute interim tests created for each subject and grade level addresses 10 specific curricular aims. You and your committee are currently trying to decide whether to recommend adoption of these new interim tests. A district policy requires that no schoolwide instructional or assessment materials are to be adopted without formal, secret-ballot approval by at least two-thirds of a school's teachers and administrators.

At the last meeting of your committee, you reviewed a validity argument in support of adopting the new interim tests. Today, the focus is on the interim tests' reliability. The district task force has supplied evidence indicating that the average internal consistency reliability coefficients, for all 12 of the interim tests, hovered close to .90. For several of the tests, the internal consistency reliability coefficient reached .95. The summary of reliability evidence provided to you was accompanied by a strong supportive statement attesting to the reliability of the new interim tests.

What would you recommend to the other members of your school's Assessment Tools Committee regarding the reliability evidence for the new interim tests? Would you supply a positive or negative recommendation, and why?

....

JIM'S DECISION

Had I been a member of the Assessment Tools Committee, I would have urged caution regarding these high, almost glistening reliability coefficients. That's because these new interim tests are clearly intended to supply instructionally actionable results for teachers—results permitting teachers to focus their instruction on alleviating specific student short-comings. But when a test's internal consistency reliability coefficients are so very high, around .90, we must conclude that the interim tests are composed of remarkably homogeneous items. Putting it differently, the items on a given interim test appear to be measuring the same thing. Tests capable of providing separate inferences about students' strengths and weaknesses would have yielded much lower internal-consistency estimates. Given what's going on with reliability, the provision of interim-test results that support teacher's focused instructional decisions is remote. The type of reliability evidence being sought in this exercise does not match the avowed instructional mission of the new interim tests.

The fundamental strategy being employed in this example is a reasonable one. The chief refinement in the approach, however, would be to employ a consistency-determination tactic better matched to the intended use of the new tests.

For the Truly Time-Pressed

Here is a quick summary of the emphasized elements of the chapter's highlighted understanding, beginning with a reposting:

The Reliability Understanding

Assessment reliability, the consistency with which a test measures whatever it measures, is represented by three conceptually different kinds of evidence, and it should be reported for both test-taker groups and individual test-takers.

* * * * *

The features of this understanding stressed in the preceding pages were (1) the synonymous nature of reliability and consistency, (2) the three different sorts of reliability evidence, (3) and the need to supply reliability evidence for both solo and group test-takers. I devoted by far the most words to the different kinds of reliability evidence because it's the source of the most reliability-related stumbling in our schools. If the kind of reliability evidence accompanying a test does not coincide with the intended use of that test, then the value of that reliability evidence— an inherently righteous and praiseworthy commodity—will evaporate.

4 FAIRNESS IN TESTING

It's About Time!

In the United States, we have been using large-scale standardized tests for more than a century and teacher-made classroom tests for twice that long. Yet, it's only recently that we have made serious efforts to eradicate unfairness in our educational assessments.

This is puzzling, because educators, like most people, favor fairness. It's a value that's espoused in essentially all cultures on earth. And given that education is mostly aimed at young people, who bear the impact of their elders' educational decisions, the need for educators to be consummately fair is unarguable.

A Barely Heard Alarm Bell Goes Off

Presumably, educators have always cared about the quality of their tests—particularly the tests they create for use in their own classes. Socrates presumably polished the tests that he personally whomped up for Plato, and Plato engaged in similar presumptive test-polishing with the tests he built for Aristotle.

Just as we believe that teachers through the ages have routinely endeavored to create flaw-free tests, we similarly believe that the assessment companies behind large-scale standardized tests also try to create high-quality products. So, in years past, whenever shortcomings were spotted in educational tests, it was generally assumed that whoever had developed the test, whether a classroom teacher or a commercial test-builder, had just goofed. People make mistakes! We used to overlook mistakes spotted in educational tests the way we overlook the occasionally misspelled word in e-mails from friends; if there was a messed-up item or two, it was no big deal. The reason it was no big deal, I'd argue, is that for most of the 20th century, truly *significant* consequences were rarely linked to students' test performances.

Then educational accountability rumbled onto the scene, accompanied by the advocacy of a new kind of large-scale accountability tests. Almost overnight there were heightened concerns about the fairness of educational testing—soon followed by calls to examine the testing tools that were being used to arrive at high-stakes decisions not only about students, but also about the teachers who taught those students.

The Historical Turn

It all began with the passage of the Elementary and Secondary Education Act (ESEA) of 1965, a federal statute providing substantial funding to support public schools—schools that, previously, had been financed almost entirely by state and local tax dollars. This law, and its accompanying fiscal largesse, was quite unprecedented. Critics began voicing concerns about whether all these new federal tax-dollars would be well spent by American educators.

Accordingly, led by Robert F. Kennedy, who was then the junior U.S. senator from New York, a host of ESEA-implementation regulations focusing on program evaluation were adopted for the new ESEA statute. These regulations, operationalizing the law itself, called for recipients of the new federal funds to evaluate *this year's* funded programs as a precondition for securing *next year's* funding. Those evaluation requirements quickly transformed ESEA into an *accountability* law.

The heart of the law's accountability requirements called for states and districts to supply formal program evaluations based chiefly on annually collected *assessment evidence* of increased student achievement. A profoundly important nationally accepted commitment had been born: the commitment to evaluate the quality of educational programs based on students' achievement test scores. That commitment survives to this day.

Most states tried to satisfy ESEA's test-focused evaluation requirements by administering standardized achievement tests of at the end of each school year in all ESEA-designated grades (grades 3–8) and once in high school. Students' performances on those tests were then used by policymakers and the general public to make evaluative judgments about the quality of federally supported programs at the local or state level.

It was not too much of a jump for some states' authorities to begin using these annual achievement tests for other purposes. The most popular of those other purposes was to use students' test scores as a reflection of students' overall achievement. Numerous states, for example, began to link the awarding of high school diplomas to students who had passed what soon became known as *minimum competency tests*. By tying high school graduation to students' displayed mastery of at least rudimentary reading, writing, and math skills, state officials hoped to head off the awarding of what critics were beginning to describe as "counterfeit diplomas." In other states, grade-to-grade promotions were sometimes made dependent on students' scoring sufficiently well on end-of-year accountability tests—so that low-scoring students were held back at lower grade levels. "High-stakes" testing for individual students had truly arrived. It is against this backdrop that educators first became aware of the potential for unfairness lurking in their most important educational tests.

In states where students' annual accountability test performances could trigger significant decisions about individual test-takers, it soon became routine to analyze statewide test score data according to such variables as gender, race, or socioeconomic status. And what came to light from these analyses was that substantial differences often existed in the success rates of different subgroups. Relentlessly, the problem of test bias began to draw more attention.

The Landmark Promotion: Two Become Three

There was one more significant event that stepped up the quest for assessment fairness: the decision by the editors of the 2014 edition of the *Joint Standards* (AERA et al., 2014) to place fairness in a position of equal importance to the long-worshipped measurement concepts of validity and reliability.

"Fairness in Testing" now has its very own chapter in the most influential book in the assessment kingdom. Moreover, early in that chapter, we see why substantial attention should be given to this issue:

… to emphasize that fairness to all individuals in the intended population of test-takers is an overriding, foundational concern, and that common principles apply in responding to test-taker characteristics that could interfere with the validity of test score interpretation. (AERA et al., 2014. p. 49)

It's official. Recognizing fairness as "an overriding, foundational concern" *capable of distorting* "the validity of test score interpretation" is an essential aspect of assessment literacy. By now you know just how seriously we must take anything that threatens to interfere with the validity of test score interpretation. Without assessment validity, testing is meaningless, and the scores it generates are incapable of doing much good.

What better way to dig into the concept of fairness in testing than to begin wrestling with this chapter's highlighted assessment understanding?

The Fairness Understanding

Fairness in educational testing is as important as validity
and reliability in the creation and evaluation of tests,
and it must be carefully documented—when practicable—
with both judgmental and empirical evidence.

* * * * *

Understanding the Understanding

Reread the Fairness Understanding, and one significant insight leaps
to the forefront: fairness in educational testing is now a primary concern, not a secondary one, meaning it cannot be an afterthought when
developing or evaluating educational tests, be they large-scale or
classroom-based.

As Figure 4.1 highlights, the understanding calls for two types of evidence to document a test's fairness, namely, *judgmental* and *empirical*
evidence.

FIGURE 4.1 | Fairness-Determination Evidence

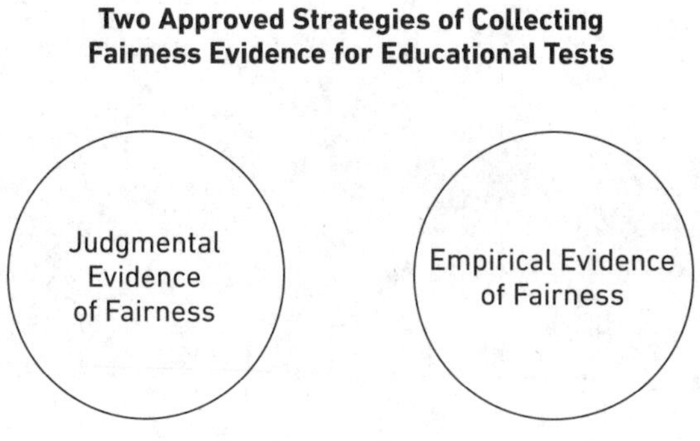

**Two Approved Strategies of Collecting
Fairness Evidence for Educational Tests**

Judgmental
Evidence
of Fairness

Empirical Evidence
of Fairness

We'll get into what's involved with those two sorts of evidence soon,
but first I'll ask you to focus on the phrase *when practicable*. Note that it's

practicable, not *practical.* Your otherwise plainspoken author has good reason for such etymological specificity. According to my dictionary, the term *practicable* means "capable of being put into practice with the available means." Whereas *practical* means "useful," *practicable* means "feasible" or "doable."

As you will soon see, the collection of one of the two sorts of evidence that might be employed to document an educational test's fairness is sometimes—in a specific real-world setting—essentially *infeasible.* By accepting the need for practicability when collecting a test's fairness evidence, educators will become inclined to adopt a relentlessly *accomplishable* approach. As you consider the nature of judgmental and empirical evidence of fairness in the remainder of this chapter, see if you believe one of those two strategies is inherently more practicable.

Judgmental Evidence of Test Fairness

If a test is composed of *items* that are biased, then the test itself will be biased. That is, it will not measure fairly. And this is why judging the fairness of test items demands our attention. If we can spot unfair items, then revise them or discard them, the modified test is almost certain to be fairer than the original version. Happily, there are effective ways to spot bias with both large-scale assessments and classroom-focused, teacher-made tests. We'll look at those procedures now.

Judging bias in large-scale assessments

Judgmental scrutiny for bias in large-scale assessment usually involves the assembly of a *bias review committee,* composed of representatives of any subgroups thought capable of being adversely affected by a test containing biased items. Generally, this means racial and ethnic minority groups, such as Latino or black Americans, or members of minority religious faiths, such Muslims. Because gender bias is sometimes found in educational tests, bias review committees also need to include reasonable representations of both males and females. Typically, a bias review committee consists of between 10 and 30 members.

There is nothing particularly exotic about the way a bias review committee operates. After an introductory orientation describing the upcoming item review task—an orientation that describes the nature of the judgments required along with the judgment of a few practice items, the committee undertakes a systematic *item-by-item* review of all the items in a potential item pool. Typically, they evaluate 10 to 15 items at a time, and there are periodic opportunities for group discussion of any items that seem to warrant additional consideration. These discussions sometimes detect lurking bias and spark reconsideration of the items involved.

The item-by-item review involves considering both the potential *offensiveness* of each and whether an item might *unfairly penalize* certain examinees. An item might offend a certain subgroup of students, for example, if it included a disparaging remark about that subgroup's ancestry or made a stereotypical assumption about that subgroup. If an item offends a student because of the item's insensitive or inaccurate depiction of that student's religion or race, the offended student is apt to perform less well on subsequent items because of an adverse emotional response to the offensive item. An item might unfairly penalize certain students if it contained content that is more likely known by members of only certain subgroups and might give them an advantage in discerning the item's answer. Clearly, if a test item features content centered on the preparation of kosher meals, Jewish students in a class ought to have an edge over other non-Jewish students.

Over the years, I have moderated many of these bias review committee meetings, and the phrasing of an item review query I have grown particularly fond of is the following (to which bias reviewers would respond for each item with a *Yes*, a *No*, or a *Not Sure*):

> *Might this item offend or unfairly penalize any group of students because of personal characteristics such as gender, ethnicity, religion, or race?*

The specific language in this judgmental charge to bias reviewers is important. Note, for example, the query's first word: *might*. If that word were *will* instead of *might*, can you see how different the reviewer's task and the resulting judgments would be? To respond *Yes* to the *will* version of this query, a reviewer must be *certain* that an item will offend or unfairly penalize; the result would be identification of fewer items as potentially biased.

Not all bias reviews are equal. Some, perhaps those conducted by a test development vendor looking to minimize the number of items denounced as biased, are almost laughably soft. Accordingly, if you are ever asked to look over the results of a judgmental review of a test's item, you should *not* assume that all such reviews are conducted with identical degrees of evaluative stringency. To discern how rigorous a bias review of a test's items has been, you really need to form your own judgments about a particular bias review procedure's toughness. Read through the language employed in the orientation directions given to reviewers; then reach your own conclusion about the procedure's rigor.

Yes, these directions are typically available for your review, along with summary results of the reviewers' judgments in whatever technical reports accompany an important educational test. If a test is still being developed, authorized individuals (such as school board members or high-ranking educational administrators) can typically analyze the items under consideration themselves. In many item-by-item bias reviews, the reviewers supply a brief written note indicating the reason they deemed individual items to be biased. Digging through these explanations is an illuminating experience. Sometimes your own judgment of particular items will diverge from those of the official reviewers, leaving you to reflect on the differences between items that you believe to be truly biased and those whose fairness you think has been improperly maligned. Even bias review panelists can make mistakes. It's an unavoidable reality of this and all other judgment-based endeavors.

Judging bias in smaller-scale and self-created assessments

It may not be standard practice for school-based educators to scrutinize the classroom tests they use or create for bias via per-item analyses, but it could be—and I'd argue that it often should be. As we'll explore in Chapter 6, the instructional decisions teachers make in the classroom, based on performance data elicited from classroom tests, are the decisions with the greatest power to support or hinder student learning. It's essential that the assessment instruments teachers deploy to make the covert overt do not distort the pictures of student status they present.

Judging potential bias in classroom tests might involve corralling a colleague or two who would be willing to review a current or under-development classroom test, look at each item, and ask: *Might this item offend or unfairly penalize any groups of students because of personal characteristics such as gender, ethnicity, religion, or race?*

Obviously, teachers who choose to employ this kind of modest-review model can pick some insights regarding potentially biased items and address those that will lead to unfair measurement. It's an immediate win. But there's an additional, long-term benefit to making item review for bias a regular practice. Knowing that the test they create will reviewed on an item-by-item basis will encourage teachers to become more aware of unintended bias, more attentive to the phrasing of their test items, and more conscientious about avoiding items that might offend or unfairly penalize their student—and thus, interfere with sound instructional decision making.

Empirical Evidence of Test Fairness

The second kind of test-fairness evidence that can provide insight into a test's evenhandedness is empirical analyses of the per-item performances of the subgroups taking a test. In brief, this approach boils down to a per-item contrast in the success rates of different subgroups of students. If, for instance, Item 32 on a grade-to-grade promotion test in reading was answered correctly by 86 percent of 3rd grade boys but only 61 percent of 3rd grade girls, then we ought to take a gander at Item 32 to see if it contains content that might give 3rd grade boys an advantage over 3rd grade girls. If so, it will need a rewrite.

The *p*-value approach

When educational assessment specialists first began getting into the detection of potential bias in test items, they simply compared the p-*values* of different student subgroups on the same item. A *p*-value is the percent of test-takers who answer an item correctly. Thus, high *p*-values (.85 or .95) are usually seen to represent easier items, while low *p*-values (.35 or .45) are regarded as tougher items. In passing, I should note that *p*-values can also reflect on the instructional expertise of the teacher who taught the student test-takers A *p*-value of .96 might reflect mastery of a very difficult but marvelously taught concept. If the average *p*-values for different subgroups of students on a test (or on a distinctive subset of items in that test) are strikingly different, this then suggests either that there may be bias lurking or that the subgroups had received meaningfully dissimilar instruction.

The DIF analysis approach

In recent years the empirical procedure of choice for contrasting the per-item performance of individual items has become something called *differential item functioning* (DIF). Such DIF analyses represent a more sophisticated process for doing what used to go on when per-item contrasts were made with the *p*-values of different subgroups. A DIF analysis, because it invokes a more detailed multi-step statistical approach, accomplishes this difficulty-contrast job far better. Nonetheless, at bottom, DIF analyses simply tell us whether, for a given group of test-takers, a given item is displaying "out-of-whackness" as answered by one subgroup versus other subgroups. Think of DIF analyses as ritzied-up contrasts in items' *p*-values.

Although statisticians differ on the necessary number of responses needed per item for decent DIF analyses, many of them urge using 500 or 1,000 test-takers per subgroup as a minimum. Some assessment specialists advocate reliance on as few as 250 test-takers per analyzed subgroup. Putting it simply, even with respect to widely used bias detection procedures such as DIF analyses, different statisticians hold different views.

The trouble with empirical evidence

If *p*-value comparisons or DIF analyses detect items that warrant another look, they are judgmentally reconsidered using a second scrutiny for biased content, then revised to eliminate any bias detected. However, if a closer look at items flagged during *p*-value comparisons or DIF analyses reveals no obvious bias in item phrasing or content, these items should *not* be sent scurrying to a shredder. That is, those items should be left in the item pool. Here's why.

Sometime disparities in the apparent difficulties of items stem more from inadequacies in the instruction supplied to the student test-takers than to any assessment bias present in an item. An important rule to guide your thinking on this issue is that *disparities in subgroup performances of an item do not automatically signify the presence of assessment bias* in that item. What it may be identifying is inadequacy in the quality of instruction provided to certain subgroups of students.

The truth is that it's difficult to definitively deem an item as being biased. But who said the building of fair educational assessments was easy? Just use your best judgment in considering each item and decide whether an observed disparity seems to be more associated with an item's unfairness or with instruction's unfairness. There's no quantifiable formula available to help you when making your "best judgment" about whether subgroup dissimilarities in an item's performance are attributable to bias or to differences in subgroup instruction. What you need to remember is that *either* of those culprits could be afoot.

We've touched already on another definite constraint on the use of empirical item analyses in bias detection. It's the fact that *a substantial number of test-takers* are required for us to undertake DIF analyses or even the less elaborate *p*-value contrasts. While it's reasonable for test publishers to muster large groups of test-takers and assemble this evidence, and while it makes sense for appointed task forces of educators to scrutinize the empirical evidence of fairness provided for all the tests considered for adoption, the approach is obviously infeasible for teacher-created tests.

As a practical matter, then, when classroom teachers, individually or in teams, set out to scrub the assessment bias out of their own teacher-made tests, empirically based bias detection procedures are a nonstarter. It makes far more sense to stick to the judgment-based procedures articulated earlier. It's the practicable approach.

A Potpourri of Fairness Notions

All children are special in their own way, but when we center our attention on the fairness of educational testing, we cannot overlook the need to be fair to those youngsters who qualify for special education services due to cognitive, emotional, or physical differences. In recent decades, U.S. educators, spurred to action by the lobbying of parents, have done a praiseworthy job of alerting assessors to the challenges of testing students with special needs. Whereas, in years past, representatives of the special education community were only called in for comment after a test had been put to bed, now large-scale test development includes the early and ongoing involvement of advocates and assessment specialists concerned with making our educational tests fairer for *all* students.

Taking up the charge to attend more closely to the fairness of tests means educators have had to wrestle with several almost-technical concepts. We'll look quickly at three that are very commonly used in connection with fairness promotion efforts: *accessibility, universal design,* and *accommodation.*

Accessibility

Accessibility, a descriptive term endorsed in the *Joint Standards,* refers to the need to ensure test-takers have an unobstructed opportunity to demonstrate their prowess regarding whatever is being assessed. To illustrate, when students who possess limited English skills are asked, in English, to show how much they know about mathematics, their lack of English can prevent them from understanding the directions and, thus, obstruct their opportunity to display their mathematical abilities. They might deploy the wrong formula, use the wrong process, or skip the item altogether. In short, test items that are inaccessible to some students will generate bad data regarding those students' true covert status.

Educators must be on guard to detect and, when practicable, excise accessibility-limiting factors in the tests we use.

Universal design

A second recently accepted notion by assessment specialists—one that's definitely worth attending to when considering test fairness—is *universal design*. Also recommended in the *Joint Standards*, universal design within assessment focuses on building educational tests in a way that will maximize accessibility for all students. "Well, of course," you might think, but for most of the history of educational testing, test-makers have considered potential accessibility challenges only at the *end* of the test development process, after the product is essentially finished. Test developers might have given some items a minor massage to make them more palatable to, or usable by, special subgroups of students. Adherence to universal design, as you might readily infer, leads to test developers' early and constant attention to test fairness.

Accommodation

Finally, attention to assessment fairness now involves various versions of *accommodation*. Accommodations are adjustments made at any point in the measurement process to provide students with a fair opportunity to respond to a test *without altering the fundamental nature of what's being assessed*. To illustrate, a possible accommodation for the math students with limited English might be a version of the test in a language that they do understand well. This step would not alter the mathematics task; it would simply remove a barrier to engaging with it. Similarly, if a student were visually impaired to the degree that the "normal-sized" letters would be unrecognized in a reading test, then substantially increasing the point size of a test's items would represent an appropriate accommodation. Again, the adjustment does not compromise the fundamental nature of the reading test.

What if this student's teacher read the items in a reading test aloud? Well, while that would make the item accessible, it would not be an appropriate accommodation because it would transform what was initially a reading test into a listening test—a significant distortion of the construct being assessed. Accommodations should increase measurement accessibility but not meaningfully muck up the nature of what's being measured.

Looking back, then, we see that this chapter's oft-acclaimed Fairness Understanding urges educators to foster fairness not only because it is the right thing to do, but also because the leaders of the educational assessment community have formally supported such an acclamation in the latest edition of the *Joint Standards* (AERA et al., 2014), the most influential published guidelines for the building and evaluating of educational tests. In addition to the important task of enhancing test fairness via the use of judgmental and empirical procedures to identify and excise or correct a test's biased items, a focus on such notions as accessibility, universal design, and accommodation can also support the reduction of assessment bias.

The Understanding's Application

Time to check in on your readiness to apply the Fairness Understanding.

As you may know, almost all 50 states have appointed a technical advisory committee (TAC) to offer the state department of education's staff members advice about assessment matters. These TACs typically meet in person two or three times a year, as well as by telephone or online if a time-sensitive assessment issue arises. State officials are free to accept or reject their state TAC's advice, but federal assessment guidelines strongly encourage states to establish and consider the views of such advisory groups.

Through the years, I have served as a member of several such TACs and, as I was writing this chapter—almost to the specific day when I initially bashed out the first version of this paragraph—I served on a TAC faced with the need to supply advice on the situation I'll describe next. Yes, that's right: this chapter's application exercise is real, not imagined! This is exciting, no?

In this Unnamed Mystery State's recently concluded state legislative session, a statute was passed with the clear intention of making a high school student's receipt of a diploma less directly dependent on passing an annually administered state-created standardized test. Under the new law, a student who fails any content area on the state test can still earn a high school diploma by passing an objectively scoreable, district-developed test that's "comparable in rigor" to the annual state test. What the state's lawmakers were trying to do, or so it seemed to me, was to provide the state's high school students with a "level playing field"; that is, the state legislature was attempting to ensure those students had a fair chance to earn their high school diplomas. Clearly, if the diploma-denial tests used in certain jurisdictions were gobs harder to pass than those tests used in other districts, fairness would be absent.

For purposes of the chapter's exercise, please assume that you are a member of this state's TAC. Assume, too, that you and your TAC colleagues are currently dealing with how best to provide data showing that these new district-developed graduation tests will be comparable in rigor to the state test.

One requirement for the "graduation tests" you're currently considering is whether the test-makers must provide *both* judgmental and empirical evidence concerning the presence of bias within the test items. Numerous local education leaders have urged the state to require *only* judgmental evidence and not demand empirical evidence. They argue that many of the state's districts are far too small, and that the collection of empirical evidence regarding potential item bias would be well beyond their resources—both financial and in terms of the number of assessment-savvy individuals capable of carrying out the necessary empirical analyses.

Another set of advocates are pushing for both empirical *and* judgmental evidence, arguing that only the collection of *empirical* evidence of items' bias, along with judgmental evidence, give the district-developed tests a chance of being deemed "comparable in rigor" to the state's standardized test (which is accompanied by both types of evidence).

Referring once more to the Fairness Understanding, would you recommend enacting a state regulation requiring the collection of both judgmental and empirical evidence of item bias? What sort of argument could you muster to support your position?

....

JIM'S DECISION

The Mystery State's upcoming TAC meeting on this specific issue is still four days away, so as I write this, I do not know how the rest of my TAC cohorts are going to come down on this real-world issue, nor do I know how the state's officials and its state school board will ultimately decide what to do. But, with those evasions plopped on the table, I can still tell you what my own recommendation would be—and why.

After reviewing the Fairness Understanding once more, please ponder for an extra few seconds the word practicable, *as it underlies my recommendation. Realistically, small districts do not have sufficient numbers of students to mount a meaningful collection and analysis of students' actual per-item performances to permit local educators to make sense out of the results. There are just too few kids to come up with sufficiently accurate statistics reflecting, for example, per-item performance disparities among diverse racial or religious subgroups. Perhaps we might find sufficient students to carry out DIF analyses on the basis of gender in some mid-size districts, but remember that at least 250 respondents are needed per subgroup (that is, 250 students must respond to the same test item), so this will usually preclude almost all DIF subgroup contrasts of interest.*

What makes more sense is for the local districts to try to do an impeccable job of collecting sound judgmental evidence of per-item assessment bias. It is often possible to employ small-sample fairness data not only for decision-making judgments but also to spur more insightful discussion by a judgmentally focused bias review committee. The mission of such small-scale empirical evidence should be catalytic, not conclusive. I'd recommend doing the best job possible in assembling the most illuminating practicable evidence regarding per-item assessment bias. For small-enrollment settings, the evidence of most worth is almost always judgmental—not empirical.

For the Truly Time-Pressed

Now it is chapter wrap-up time, with a super-skinny summary of the chapter's much beloved understanding:

The Fairness Understanding

Fairness in educational testing is as important as validity and reliability in the creation and evaluation of tests, and it must be carefully documented—when practicable—with both judgmental and empirical evidence.

* * * * *

The big takeaways are that (1) test fairness is officially a big deal—as important a concern in assessment as the traditional heavyweights of validity and reliability, (2) there should ideally be two kinds of evidence assembled to document test fairness, (3) but only when getting both kinds of evidence is practicable.

When it's not possible to the get sufficiently large samples of responses to represent all student subgroups who must be considered, getting *empirical evidence* isn't feasible. It isn't feasible either in individual school districts, or in individual classrooms, grade-level teams, or high school departments. In all these settings, and with the tests used there or created to be used there, educators must rely solely on *judgmental evidence* to detect bias. This means scrutinizing test items, asking whether bias might be present, taking corrective steps to ensure the quality of their tests and, in doing so, increasing educators' chances of making better educational decisions.

SCORE REPORTS

Information That Supports Action

Whenever someone asks me for a serious judgment about the quality of a particular standardized test, my initial response is almost always the same: I ask to see how the test's scores are reported. That's right—the best way to get a fast fix on a test's worth is usually to look at the score report being used to describe a test-taker's performance.

To recognize why a standardized test's score reports are so indicative of its quality, you need only to recall the reason educators test students in the first place. We test to arrive at accurate—that is, *valid*—inferences about students' unseen knowledge and skills. Then we go on to use those valid score-based inferences about what students know and don't yet know, and about what they can and can't yet do, to make more enlightened decisions about our instructional next steps. Figure 5.1 illustrates the action sequence of assessment-abetted education.

Note that we formulate and implement actions only *after* we have reviewed the results of a test. In the case of large-scale standardized tests, those results are presented in score reports. And, as the figure illustrates, if we can't make sufficient sense out of a standardized test's score reports, then the entire sequence stops dead in its tracks. Putting it as directly as possible, if testing does not make a direct contribution to improving the decisions educators make about students, testing is a waste of time, and we shouldn't bother with it. However, if the score reports are properly illuminating, their worth cannot be overstated.

FIGURE 5.1 | Assessment-Abetted Education: The Usual Sequence

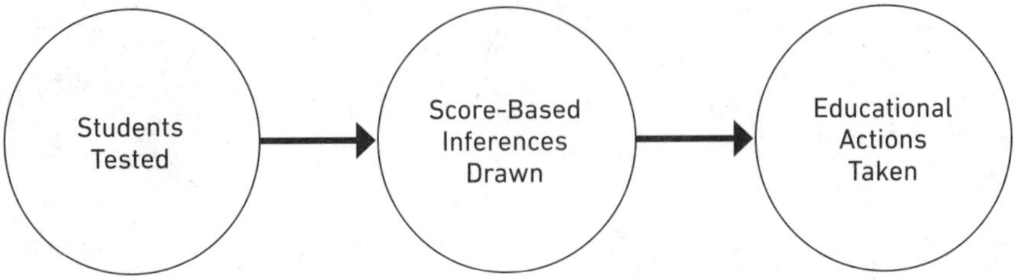

This chapter focuses on the great value that score reports from large-scale standardized tests, such as nationally standardized college admission exams or statewide accountability tests, can bring to the educational enterprise. Although classroom tests are not the emphasis here, some of the notions we will discuss have implications for classroom teachers, who can often benefit from rethinking how best to report results of the tests they create and use with their own students.

Purposive Actionability

The assessment topic we're about to explore draws from the underlying interrelationships among educational measurement's most important concepts and procedures. First, there's the Validity Understanding which, you will recall, requires (1) that the score-based interpretations about test-takers be accurate and (2) that those interpretations support the intended use of the test. It makes sense, then, that test results need to be reported in such a way as to engender *actionability*. Here's what I mean:

- If the test's mission is to *make comparisons among test-takers*, we need score reports that facilitate those comparisons by presenting clearly contrastable reports of students' performances at the levels of generality most needed for action, typically, student-by-student, school-by-school, or district-by-district comparisons.
- If the test's mission is to *improve ongoing instruction and learning*, we need score reports that provide detailed information about students' pinpointed content mastery at "grain sizes"—that is, at

levels of generality most useful to teachers planning their next-step instruction or to students planning their next-step learning.

• If the test's mission is to *evaluate the quality of instruction*, we need score reports that supply readily comprehensible depictions of how well students performed at the various levels of interest—for instance, student, class, school, or district.

Fortunately, the intended purposes of standardized tests are almost always on the record. Less fortunately, accessing "the record" can require a little effort. Although it would be easy enough for every standardized test's score report to include a brief statement of its measurement mission, this is not a widespread practice. Consider the marketing incentive that commercial test development firms have to dodge the test-purpose issue. If a test is assumed to be suitable for all sorts of purposes, it becomes attractive to the widest range of potential purchasers.

At any rate, to track down a test's intended purpose, it's usually necessary to go to the technical report or "technical manual" associated with that test. If a test is administered by state education authorities, the technical report is often posted on the state's Department of Education website. In some instances, information about a test's intended uses can be snared online from a test's publisher. Often, however, a test's intended usage is laid out in very general terms. The really important thing is for a score report to mesh with the specific purpose for which a particular test is to be used in a particular situation. If you're a middle school teacher who wants a set of test results to inform your decisions about if and how to modify some of your instructional strategies, then hyper-general score reports contrasting students in different nations will be of scant use to you.

Once we have a reasonably accurate idea of the measurement mission of a standardized test—whether it be comparative, instructional, or evaluative—the next step is to judge the degree to which the reported results are actionable in accord with that mission. For example, suppose the primary purpose of a statewide standardized test is documented as *instructional*. In front of you, you have a score report for the ELA portion of the test, and it provides the results for identifiable subsets of items related to specific, instructionally addressable curricular targets. An example of such a target might be "identification of a passage's inferred, unstated, main idea." The question to ask now is whether there are enough items linked to this curricular aim to permit a teacher to make reasonably accurate inferences about a student's mastery of that aim. (We'll consider the question of how many items are "enough" in a bit.) If there *are* enough items, you would judge this aspect of the score report to be satisfactory. It supplies decision-relevant evidence in clear support of the test's chief purpose. In other words, a teacher reviewing a student's performance on the collection of items measuring the skill of inferring a main idea can start to think about what sort of instructional action might be taken in light of the covert status now revealed.

Whether a test has an instructional mission, as our example does, or a comparative or evaluative mission, its score report must provide sufficient information to guide warranted action taking, and such action taking must be in accord with the test's official measurement mission. Accordingly, we arrive at this chapter's assessment understanding:

The Score Report Understanding

Because inferences about students are based on test-takers' score reports, users must demand that results be easily interpreted in accord with the test's intended use.

* * * * *

With a few exceptions, classroom educators have traditionally had little influence on the formulation of a standardized test's score reports. Yes, sometimes an advisory group of teachers offers suggestions about score reports during construction of a state's accountability tests. Yet, in most instances, the crafting of score reports falls to the assessment specialists working for the test publisher. These reports come to teachers from the district office or directly from the assessment vendor. Typically, this means that educators will be playing a reactive role regarding a score report's usefulness. This chapter's understanding argues that action should replace such passivity. It asserts that teachers should demand score reports fashioned in a way that's truly useful for the people who are called on to use them.

In fairness, most makers of standardized tests aren't venomous villains; they really do care about children and how well they are being educated. Nor are they motivated solely by the prospect of selling lots of tests to boost profits and increase market share. However, business realities underscore the potential impact that a few strongly voiced concerns from a handful of thoughtful educators can have. We have the power to reduce shortcomings in a score-reporting procedure. We can and should wield that power. But first, we need a clear idea of what we want.

Understanding the Understanding

If you look closely at the Score Report Understanding, you'll see that it opens with a reason and closes with two demands. That's three components to consider. Here we go.

Engendering Actionable Inferences

Maybe some teachers test just for the fun of it, but I never did. By and large, teachers test to find out what their students know and can do. We test to arrive at sufficiently accurate interpretations of their knowledge and skills so that we can make good decisions about what and how to teach them. Even standardized testing—or at least a great deal of it—is claimed to help educators teach kids better.

Take standardized achievement tests, which are designed to measure what students have learned. When they are deployed in schools, it's to get a fix on students' status with respect to the most important curricular aims being pursued. Accordingly, the way these tests' scores are reported is *integral* to the educative process.

Please note that a good score report from a standardized test need not and should not communicate precisely what instructional actions ought to be taken with particular students. There is a huge array of instructional tactics available to teachers and countless variables to consider, from a given teacher's talents and style to the class composition and individual students' optimal learning approaches. What a well-designed score report from a standardized test *should* communicate clearly are not the means of instruction but the suitable, clarified ends to guide next-step instructional choices. If a teacher's students are flopping on a particular component of what's being assessed, it's generally the teacher's job to come up with an instructional amelioration approach.

Interpretability: Far Easier Said Than Done

With a firm grasp of the *why* behind score reports, let's delve into what makes a good one. The first demand set out in this chapter's understanding is that score reports be "easily interpretable." What does this mean?

Almost all of today's standardized tests report student performance data in one of three ways: (1) using *percentiles*, (2) using *scale scores*, and (3) using *performance-level categories*. Let's consider each of these reporting techniques briefly—dodging measurement jargon whenever feasible.

Percentiles

Reporting test scores via percentiles has been with us for at least a century, probably much longer. Moreover, few of today's grown-ups have not been on the receiving end of at least a few standardized tests' score-report percentiles. So, it's not surprising that most educators understand when a test-taker earns a *raw score* of, for example, 38 points on a 50-point test, the test-taker's 76 *percent correct* would *not* be the same as that test-taker's *percentile*.

A percentile indicates the percent of test-takers that the individual test-taker outperformed. It's determined by comparing that test-taker's raw score to the scores of a representative group of prior test-takers—what's typically called a *norm group*. Depending on the performances of students in the norm group, a raw score of 38 points on a 50-point quiz might fall at the 92nd percentile, the 82nd, the 79th, or some other percentile. We interpret the meaning of a student's score by "referencing" it back to the norm group's performances. Reporting through percentiles is sometimes called *norm-referenced measurement* for this reason.

One trouble with these generally well-understood percentiles, though, is that they do not lend themselves to many of the routine statistical machinations that must be performed on students' test scores in order to provide readily understandable syntheses of test-takers' performances. You see, for many years we have used percentiles to represent different students' relative performances on the same set of items in a fixed-form test. Yet, an increasing number of today's standardized tests are *computer-based* (computer-administered and computer-scored) or *computer-adaptive* (wherein item difficulty adjustments are made during the test, based on the test-taker's responses to earlier items in the test). In short, different students actually end up responding to different sets of items. As a consequence, despite the intuitive understandability of percentiles, they cannot be employed in the complex statistical analyses often required for the reporting of such scores.

Scale scores

As you may remember from Chapter 2, a scale score is simply a raw score (the number of items a student answered correctly) *after* this raw score has been transformed by a conversion to a new numerical scale.

The procedure is a little confusing to describe but relatively straightforward to conduct, especially if you are a statistician. The test-takers' raw scores are manipulated statistically so that they are suitable for the sorts of analyses that *can't* be performed using percentiles. Thus, for example, a newly installed score scale can be used to represent the achievement of students over a long period of time—say, from grade 3 all the way through grade 12. This kind of *vertical scale* has a slew of practical payoffs. It allows educators to monitor what happens to students at different grades with respect to their mastery of pivotal skills and knowledge. For instance, by employing vertical scale scores, we can tell whether specific students are keeping up with their grade-level classmates at every grade level that's tested. But these long-duration, student-specific contrasts can be pulled off only with vertically arranged scale scores, not with percentiles or raw scores.

Too many comparison-confounding elements are found in raw scores and percentiles to allow such grade-to-grade contrasts. However, when statisticians create a nifty new scale that's *specifically intended to take those confounding elements into consideration*, then we can legitimately carry out a host of educationally relevant statistical analyses. And this is why, of course, we see the score reports of so many high-stakes tests these days relying on scale scores as their chief reporting mechanism.

All of this sounds so delightful—a tale of heroic statisticians slaying an army of score-distorting dragons—that you probably expect there is a hitch coming. And there is. The annoying reality is that scale scores are as tough as the devil to understand. Suppose, for example, I informed you that the performance level you just earned on a brand-new standardized achievement test was equivalent to a scale score of 855 on a scale from 500 to 1,000. What do you think your 855 indicates? That is, what does your 855 *mean*?

The fact is that, without some sort of interpretative support for the users of score reports, a scale score is basically uninterpretable. Although scale scores can warm the cockles of a statistician's heart (whatever a cockle is), scale scores are of decisively limited value to practitioners. Even after using a particular set of scale scores for several years, educators can remain baffled by those scores. The vexing fact is that in almost all settings, scale scores are not intuitively understandable to those receiving scale-score-based reports. They are good for psychometricians who are trying to make sense out of numerous test scores—especially when those scores are being considered over a series of years—but scale scores are of far less use to real-world educators who are trying to squeeze some intuitively understandable next-step instructional implications out of a collection of students' performances on important tests. And this is why our third reporting option has recently become so popular. Let's consider it.

Performance-level reports and descriptors

Teachers have used categories to report students' test performance ever since teachers have tested students. For some reason, maybe because the alphabet was just there, teachers became very fond of linking performance categories to letters, and we wound up with the widely employed system of *A, B, C, D,* and *F.* Another popular option was just to report the number of a test's items that a student had answered correctly. Thereafter, using systems translating raw scores or percent-correct into letter-grade categories, teachers could provide their students with both a numerical score and a relative-performance categorization.

We have employed category-based reporting systems of one sort or another in the United States for a long, long time. But when the No Child Left Behind Act (NCLB) was enacted into law in early 2002, states found themselves obliged by federal statute to employ at least three categorical reporting levels to indicate how well a student had succeeded in mastering a state's "challenging" curricular aims.

Faced with this requirement, many states adopted the category designators then employed when reporting results from the federal National Assessment of Student Progress (NAEP)—a frequently administered test of basic skills given nationally at certain grade levels. Those four NAEP levels were *Advanced, Proficient, Basic,* and *Below Basic.* (Technically, the *Below Basic* designation was not an official NAEP reporting category, but it was used for the lowest scores leftover after using the other three categories.) Because of the already-widespread use of these four categories, many states' per-student reporting for NCLB either employed them or used similar descriptive labels. These reporting systems are typically referred to as *performance-level reporting systems* or *achievement-level reporting systems.*

In the same way that it's common practice to tie students' letter grades to a specified number of points earned, performance-level reports are intended to help educators interpret standardized test performances by staking out a specific range of scale scores represented by each categorical level. For example, if a scale-score range happened to be set as a 1,000-point range from 1,000 to 2,000, the reporting categories might be set up like this: *Advanced* = 1,820 and above; *Proficient* = 1,530–1,819; *Basic* = 1,529–1,280; and *Below Basic* = 1,279 and below.

To make such results more meaningful—not only to educators but also to students and their families—such scale-score systems are sometimes accompanied by *performance-level descriptors* or, as they are also called, *achievement-level descriptors*. These descriptive statements, usually a paragraph or so in length, attempt to capture in words what it means to have a score that falls into the "proficient" range, the "basic" range, and so on.

Figure 5.2 presents four categories in which levels of student performance could be reported: The levels shown are not "real" in the sense that they have been lifted intact from any one state's performance-level descriptors. Rather, they represent my melding of several states' current score-reporting procedures. Nonetheless, the resultant levels presented in the figure are quite similar to what's often used nationally.

**FIGURE 5.2 | Illustrative Performance Descriptors
                for a Flagrantly Fictitious State**

STATE ENGLISH LANGUAGE ARTS PERFORMANCE DESCRIPTORS

Explanation: Based on the scale-score earned on the end-of-year state assessment, each student's performance in ELA falls into one of the following levels.

Level 4. The student performing at this level displays *advanced* mastery of the knowledge, skills, and practices represented by the state's official content standards.

Level 3. The student performing at this level displays *proficient* mastery of the knowledge, skills, and practices represented by the state's official content standards.

Level 2. The student performing at this level displays *partial proficiency* in mastering the knowledge, skills, and practices represented by the state's official content standards.

Level 1. The student performing at this level displays clearly *inadequate proficiency* in mastering the knowledge, skills, and practices represented by the state's official content standards.

Note, for instance, that the four performance levels are reported as numbers, and the higher the number, the higher the quality of the test performance. The use of numbers rather than verbal descriptors has become increasingly popular in recent years, in part because it relieves state authorities from the responsibility of spelling out in precise detail what they mean by "basic" or "proficient." As Figure 5.2's descriptors illustrate, some states try to embed in their numerical descriptive language the very same labels that they have used in the past.

The point I'm making is that quality-descriptive practices vary. For example, the illustrative, author-manufactured set of performance-level descriptors in Figure 5.2 is linked to the imaginary state's "official" content standards—that is, the curricular aims the state's students are supposed to master. Many states do this, assuming that if educators want to know what it means to be "proficient" in a particular ELA state standard for grade 5, they will dig through the state standards' documents for the answer. Other states attempt to infuse at least some of those official curricular aims into the performance-level descriptors themselves. These descriptors can be terse or truly voluminous, reflecting an always-fruitless attempt to list completely the set of determining factors associated with a particular level of quality.

If you were to embark on an internet hunt for "state performance-level descriptors," what you'd find would be a substantial variety in the ways that states try to tie down how well a student has performed on an important state test. You'll always see an attempt to lay out some sort of *quality gradient* across the different performance levels, but the clarity embodied in those descriptions varies substantially.

And here we find our score-reporting plot thickening a mite more. Even after determining how to describe the various levels of students' performances, it is still necessary to carry out a *standard-setting study* so that we can link each performance level's descriptor to a specific score range. This task is usually carried out by a *standard-setting panel*, a group of mostly educators, and some noneducators, charged with recommending *cut-scores* that will appropriately differentiate among the performance-level categories already carved out. Although definite improvements have been made in the guidance we provide to members of standard-setting panels who undertake this challenge, at bottom the selection of cut-score ranges is still a totally *judgmental* task.

Hopefully, the score-reporting procedure I've just sketched makes sense to you. It's a process in which educators first try to spell out what's meant by each of several performance levels, from lowest to highest quality, and then employ systematic standard-setting procedures to link specific scale-score ranges to different performance levels. I have seen these standard-setting procedures carried out many times, having often moderated the deliberations of panelists attempting to link cut-score ranges to quality-level categories. Invariably, these panelists took the work seriously and summoned the very best judgments they could muster.

With *every* set of achievement-level descriptors I have seen, there is always the potential for different panelists to arrive at differing interpretations of a given description. Most words, despite our best efforts to employ them precisely, contain a smattering of squish. Even folks who took part in the actual composition of the specific performance-level descriptors being used can still end up with varied interpretations of what a description signifies.

Similarly, even the most tightly conceptualized standard-setting procedures—the steps a standard-setting panel takes to arrive at suitable cut-scores to separate students' performances into different categories—usually vary from one situation to another and are often influenced by the personalities and priorities of the empaneled.

Given the imprecisions of language and the caprices of human judgment, it is unlikely that we'll ever arrive at a totally flawless score-reporting system. The best we can hope for are well-intentioned implementations of thoughtful procedures devised to deal with an inherently messy judgmental task.

Accordance with a Test's Purpose

The Score Report Understanding clarifies that, in addition to demanding that score reports be easily interpretable, every test's score report should be consonant with the test's intended use. We'll look first at why this aspect of the understanding is so significant, then explore how to assemble credible evidence that the match between a score report and a test's purpose is a good one.

An oft-violated necessity

We're all clear that that test-based performances are educators' means of arriving at accurate inferences about students' unseen knowledge and skills—inferences that allow us to whip up winning instructional programs for them. It is the *validity* of these score-based inferences that is so crucial to the entire educational assessment enterprise—but only if these inferences, are "in accord with the test's intended use." The *Joint Standards* (AERA et al., 2014) persuasively emphasizes this requirement.

This need for accordance with purpose trips up so many educators trying to snare useful insights from a standardized test's score report. We often assume that the test we're using to try to make comparisons among test-takers was indeed designed to be *comparative;* the test we're using to try to improve instruction or learning was designed to be *instructional;* or the test we're using to evaluate our teaching prowess was designed to be *evaluative.* In most instances—that's right, in *most* instances—we are mistaken. In most instances, standardized tests do *not* do a good job in carrying out that test's intended purpose.

To illustrate, try the following two assertions on for size—assertions that I believe to be stone-cold true but that run counter to most educators' beliefs.

> *Although nationally sanctioned standards for educational testing call for evidence supporting a test's intended use, the standardized tests currently being used to evaluate our schools and teachers are largely unaccompanied by evidence that they do what they say they can.*

> *Despite frequent claims that standardized achievement tests help teachers diagnose students' strengths and weaknesses, and that such diagnosticity will engender better instruction, most of today's standardized tests yield results of no instructionally diagnostic value.*

The first of these two counterintuitive assertions is germane whenever the intended mission of a standardized test is evaluative. With almost no exceptions, the standardized tests being used these days to evaluate the instructional caliber of a school district, a school, or an individual teacher are being employed without a shred, or even a half-shred, of evidence that the tests are appropriate for this significant evaluative mission,

Turning to the second of these two counterintuitive contentions, while many of the assessment companies that create standardized tests tout their tests as being "instructionally beneficial," the score reports accompanying those tests—the reports that ostensibly contribute to instructional insights from teachers—are either far too broad or far too narrow to truly help teachers teach.

So, it becomes important to see confirmation that a test's score report supports what the test is supposed to do. Standardized educational tests that don't meet these criteria, that aren't *fit for purpose* (a useful British expression), should not be used. If you ever find yourself looking at a score report for a significant standardized test, and the test is not accompanied by evidence indicting satisfactory test-purpose match (or digital links to such evidence), then you should register a complaint with appropriate complaint-receiving governmental or political officials that something is squirrelly in Measurement Land.

What kind of evidence?

It is easier to rant about the need for persuasive evidence in support of a test's intended measurement mission than it is to collect and display such evidence. Remember, the guiding intention here is to supply convincing proof that a test will or will not provide a suitable foundation for the specified educational decisions to be made. As with so many other decisions in the "objective and quantitative" field of educational assessment, we must reach conclusions regarding a test-to-purpose match *judgmentally*. But the means of garnering this judgmental evidence should be systematic, sensible, and practicable. An example would be a panel of properly oriented educators rendering individual judgments, then summarized panel judgments, of the adequacy of a specific test-to-purpose match.

The fundamental decision on the table revolves around whether a test's reporting system is good enough *to warrant use of the test* itself. Another set of decisions relate to whether an educator should do any voice-raising—in criticism or praise—regarding the score-report system being used. If there are deficits in the score-reporting system that can be corrected, a call for modifications might lead to actual changes in the reports. And if a test's score reports are doing a super job, it makes sense to let the world know about it, so that more such reports will be provided in the future, both locally and elsewhere.

Summing up, then, the Score Report Understanding encourages those who are examining and using the score reports from standardized achievement tests to do some double-duty demanding. It prompts us to insist these reports provide readily interpretable information about students' test performances, and that this easy-to-make-sense-of information clearly supports the test's intended purpose.

The truth is that you might have a spectacular standardized test in front of you—a carefully constructed test accompanied by a host of compelling evidence of validity, reliability, and fairness. But if the test's score reporting is not actionable, it's all a colossal waste. That test cannot support sound educational decisions because the vessel for getting test results to the educators who need them will have run aground.

The Understanding's Application

Ready for your opportunity to apply the chapter's Score Report Understanding, albeit in a *let's pretend* setting?

Please pretend that you are a classroom teacher who has been appointed to serve on a 20-member statewide committee of educators asked to consider the score-reporting system that's been proposed for use next year. The reporting system is to be employed with a set of brand-new standardized reading tests for students in grades 3 through 8, created for your state by an external test development vendor. You and the other educators on your committee have spent the past two meetings learning the particulars of the new reading tests' proposed score reports.

Now your committee is wrestling with the issue of whether the proposed score reports are suitably supportive of what the test's creators identify, with barely hidden pride, as the new test's chief assessment task: "To support teachers' instructional decision making." Although local districts *may* employ this test for their own district-focused accountability purposes, it is not intended to serve any statewide evaluative function.

The score report's reporting mechanism relies on a student's status with respect to a single, overall claim: "The student can read with comprehension all grade-appropriate reading tasks." The scale scores on the 45-item reading tests are presented in relation to this claim as follows:

- *3 points* = Comprehension demonstrated completely
- *2 points* = Comprehension demonstrated partially
- *1 point* = Undemonstrated comprehension

The test's score-reporting mechanism identifies a student's status with respect to a single, overall claim, namely: "The student can read with comprehension all grade-appropriate reading tasks." Students' scale scores on the 45-item reading tests are presented, as seen above, in relation to this claim. In addition, however, because 15 items at each grade level are made publicly available for instructional purposes, the state's teachers are encouraged to garner instructional insights from how each student performed on *each* of the 15 items. A student's separate performance on all 15 of the released items is also a part of the proposed score report. (The 30 unreleased items at the various grade levels will be used each year to provide the information needed to statistically equate the difficulties of a test form's 15 new items with those of the previously released 15 items.)

In review, then, the new state-provided reading tests for grades 3 through 8 are intended to provide educators with information consistent with the test's instructional-improvement mission. The two chief ways of reporting a student's test performance are by using three claim-mastery levels as well and by supplying for each student an item-by-item performance on 15 of the 45-item test's items.

Soon, your committee will vote on the suitability of the proposed reporting system. Would you vote yay or nay? Also, please think through *why* you'd be voting this way.

···

JIM'S DECISION

Had I been casting a ballot, it would be a decisively negative one. The reason for my negativity stems from what I regard as a mismatch between the score-reporting systems and the measurement mission.

What we see here is a set of new tests intended to support teachers in their instructional efforts. Well, what teachers need when devising their instructional plans is an accurate interpretation of what students can and can't do. The proposed test has chosen two ways to report students' performances, neither of which do a first-rate job in supporting instructional decisions. If score reports are issued at the wrong descriptive level—that is, if they provide results in too broad or too narrow a form—they are difficult to use. Claim-level reporting is way too broad. A performance descriptor like "comprehension demonstrated partially" is simply too big to be instructionally useful. In an interesting contrast, the per-item reporting is way too narrow. Per-item reports are rarely used by teachers, and when they are, they're not used for very long. That's because they are not easily interpretable. It is simply too much trouble to wade through a litany of solo-item results to come up with accurate interpretations of a given student's strengths and weaknesses. Although item-by-item reporting oozes specificity and potential instructional utility, it's far too time-consuming and brain-deadening for teachers to use over the long haul—even once a year!

What I always hanker for in a score report accompanying an instructionally focused test is a manageably small set of descriptions of students' status with respect to significant, instructionally addressable lumps of content—the key skills or bodies of knowledge. If the architects of a score report are properly preoccupied with describing students' performances in ways that make sense for teachers' next-step decisions, the resultant score reports will most likely operate as intended and help teachers improve learning outcomes.

For the Truly Time-Pressed

Score reports are a critically overlooked factor in assessment's effectiveness or ineffectiveness, and they have a real impact on what educators do. This chapter's understanding explains why and lays out what's required:

The Score Report Understanding

Because inferences about students are based on test-takers' score reports, users must demand that results be easily interpreted in accord with the test's intended use.

* * * * *

As I strum the chapter's score-reporting guitar chord one final time, please remember the reality expressed in the final nine words of the Score Report Understanding. What they imply is that data for test-based inferences supporting comparative, instructional, and evaluative decisions should be provided by score reports. Indeed, if students' test scores were not reported, there'd be little reason to do any testing in the first place. Accordingly, we educators must clamor for score reports that help us interpret students' test performances. A demand for such actionable score reports will engender the building of better, purpose-supportive tests.

FORMATIVE ASSESSMENT

Ends-Means Magic

In this chapter, we will be considering formative assessment, a process featuring the *instructional* use of classroom assessments. It's an enormously effective process that works because it's an educational incarnation of the classic ends-means goal attainment strategy that humans have been using since we first trod the earth. I have no evidence to back up this historical allegation, but I stand by it; the ends-means strategy works so wonderfully well, I am certain that it always has.

To ensure we'll be in reasonable agreement about the major concepts in the chapter, let's begin with a bit of term defining.

The Essence of Ends-Means

Ends-means thinking (sometimes referred to as means-ends thinking) is widely employed when setting out to accomplish a given goal. That goal can be as simple as determining the least arduous way of tying one's shoelaces or as sophisticated as building a spacecraft to transport affluent passengers back and forth to nearby planets.

The way an ends-means strategy works is step-by-step simple:

1. Identify the desired end.
2. Select the means and implement it.
3. Evaluate the effect and, if necessary, select an alternate means.

In Step 1, the person decides on an intended outcome to be accomplished. Examples of such ends would include earning a college degree, saving enough money to buy a fuel-efficient automobile, or shedding 10 unwanted pounds prior to swimsuit season. The significance of such ends, of course, can range all over the lot. Some are important and some are not.

In Step 2, the person sets out a plan to achieve the decided-upon outcome. In most instances, this is carried out in the twinkling of an eye, typically without formally isolating a complete array of all potential means prior to selecting one. The individual sets a goal, quickly comes up with what seems to be a suitable way of achieving that goal, and then gets to work.

In Step 3, if the chosen means, once carried out, did *not* achieve the desired end, the person using the strategy decides on another means and then embarks on this alternative approach. Of course, if the selected means attained the sought-for end, that is end of story—no further action is needed.

Most of us employ this informal strategy many times a day. In a sense, ends-means thinking represents a "trial and error" approach. If a given "try" is not working, we try something new. We do this so often that we rarely recognize ends-means thinking is going on.

Ends-means thinking can also be carried out in a much more deliberative manner. As soon as a to-be-sought end has been identified (Step 1), an individual end-seeker or an end-seeking group can systematically identify a set of means that might reasonably lead to ends attainment, then carefully select the means thought most likely to work (Step 2). If the chosen means does, in fact, work, all is well. If not, then it's a matter of choosing and deploying one of the previously identified alternatives (Step 3).

A Fast Flip to Formative Assessment

When ends-means thinking is applied to instruction, particularly to classroom instruction, it's called *formative assessment.*

I've written two books on formative assessment (Popham, 2008, 2011). Because I tend to admire my own previously written views, I consulted those two books while preparing to write this chapter and found myself concurring enthusiastically with what I read. To demonstrate this concurrence tangibly, let's get this section underway with the definition of formative assessment that I offered in both of those books:

> Formative assessment is a planned process in which assessment-elicited evidence of students' status is used by teachers to adjust their ongoing instructional procedures or by students to adjust their current learning tactics. (Popham, 2008, p. 6)

As you can see from this still cherished definition, formative assessment is a *planned* process, not a spur-of-the-moment reaction. Of course, there are flexible teachers who routinely make instant, on-the-spot adjustments in their teaching based on a few students' perplexed frowns or one student's confusion-born question. These immediate instructional adjustments often pay off big-time. But such instantaneous instructional shifts, though praiseworthy, are *not* formative assessment. We'll delve deeper into this point as the chapter goes on.

Also note that, in this definition, formative assessment is a *process*, not a test. In formative assessment, we *use* tests to collect evidence about students—evidence that allows teachers (or students themselves) to adjust what they are currently doing. It is this test-garnered evidence about students' status that can lead to adjustments. Accordingly, it is a serious labeling mistake to refer to a test as "a formative assessment."

Next, notice this definition of formative assessment clarifies that when the evidence produced by classroom tests is at hand, this evidence might lead to adjustments in the way *teachers* are teaching or in the way *students* are trying to learn. It's means revision in two dimensions! Depending on what the test-elicited evidence reveals, adjustments can be made by teachers, by students, by *neither* teachers nor students, or by *both* teachers and students. Formative assessment employs classroom tests to determine *whether* any adjustments are warranted.

There's one more aspect of this definition I'd like to highlight, and it's the phrase *ongoing instructional procedures*. In formative assessment, teachers employ multiple assessment measures to gauge the success of en route instructional segments aimed at the along-the-way skills or bodies of knowledge that students need to master as they work toward a higher-level curricular goal. This reliance on evidence to determine success is the most important commonality between formative assessment and ends-means thinking. In most applications of ends-means strategies, such evidence gathering usually occurs after the full-length implementation of a set of means. In formative assessment, evidence is gathered several times as an along-the-way check on whether the instructional activities being used do or do not need to be adjusted.

In summary, and as illustrated in Figure 6.1, classroom formative assessment is a thoughtful attempt by teachers (and sometimes students) to apply an ends-means strategy to the pursuit of chosen learning outcomes.

FIGURE 6.1 | Ends-Means Thinking and the Formative Assessment Process

An Ends-Means Strategy

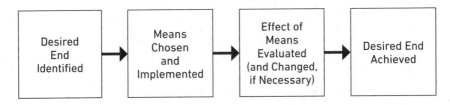

The Formative Assessment Process

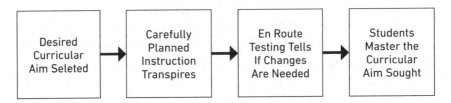

From Whence Cometh Formative Assessment?

Although Terry Crooks (1988), Ross Sadler (1989), and a few other assessment authorities wrote cogently about classroom assessment's role in supporting learning back in the 20th century and found receptive audiences in New Zealand, Australia, and the United Kingdom, before the 2002 enactment of the No Child Left Behind Act, U.S. educators' interest in formative assessment was low. That changed with NCLB's call for schools to document students' *measurable* "adequate yearly progress" or be on the receiving end of some serious federal penalties, both financial and reputational.

Feeling the federal pressure, U.S. educators undertook an earnest search for ways to improve their students' annual test scores. Happily, many of them found what seemed to be a magic bullet in a pair of journal articles published in 1998. The first article was a lengthy, rigorously conducted review of the instructional impact of classroom assessments when used *formatively* to improve teachers' instructional success. This review, covering almost 10 years' worth of empirical research, was carried out by two British researchers, Paul Black and Dylan Wiliam. It was published in a peer-refereed journal, *Assessment in Education* (Black & Wiliam, 1998a), which did not have wide readership in the United States. Commencing their review with a scrutiny of almost 700 potentially relevant research publications, Black and Wiliam identified approximately 250 solid reports, analyzed the very devil out of them, and then concluded that "the research reported here shows conclusively that formative assessment does improve learning" (p. 61). Those of us who have spent substantial time looking at research reviews, of course, tend to become quite intrigued by any reports showing that anything works *conclusively!* Later that same year, Black and Wiliam (1998b) published an essay endorsing formative assessment in the *Phi Delta Kappan*. That journal was better known to American educators, and this second article reached more American-educator eyes.

As NCLB and its score-boosting pressures took hold in the early 2000s, a certain number of these educators recalled Black and Wiliam's advocacy of test-based instructional process. This thing called "formative assessment" (whatever it was) seemed to promise a relatively low-cost way of improving students' scores on the high-stakes tests being used to evaluate schools.

Accordingly, professional development workshops were held, journal articles were written, books dealing solely with formative assessment were authored. Years passed, and additional research continued to support the efficacy of formative assessment (see, for example, Hattie & Yates, 2014). In a piece in the journal *Educational Leadership* based on five reviews of related research covering more than 4,000 investigations undertaken in the previous 40 years, Dylan Wiliam concluded that, if implemented well, "formative assessment can effectively double the speed of student learning" (2007/2008, pp. 36–37).

An instructional strategy that can double the speed of student learning is nothing at which to sneeze. And yet, despite all the accolades poured on formative assessment by educational researchers, this potent process remains astonishingly underused, particularly in the United States. This is a downright shame.

I hope, by the time you conclude your interaction with this chapter, you'll see why formative assessment has earned a spot among this book's six foundational pillars of assessment literacy. More important, I hope you'll use formative assessment yourself or advocate that others use it, too. Here, then, is the understanding featured in this chapter:

The Formative Assessment Understanding

Although currently underused, formative assessment is a remarkable, research-ratified process in which teachers and students use classroom assessments to make needed adjustments that can dramatically improve students' learning.

* * * * *

Understanding the Understanding

One of the best ways to get a solid handle on the Formative Assessment Understanding is to firm up your grasp of the formative assessment process itself.

Formative Assessment's Fundamentals

Formative assessment is a planned instructional *process* in which assessment-collected evidence is used either by teachers or by students to make any necessary adjustments in their current efforts. For teachers, usually this means a modification of either current instructional activities or those planned for upcoming classes. For students, it means adjusting their *learning tactics*—whatever procedures they are currently employing to try to learn what they are supposed to be learning. The decisions of what to adjust or not, and how to adjust it if necessary, are based on the results of classroom assessments. When we use the results of classroom assessments in this way, we are doing so in the sense that Michael Scriven (1967) advocated when he introduced the terms *formative* and *summative* to the field of educational evaluation. *Formative* evaluations, he said, focus on appraising the merits of emerging, still malleable instructional interventions. *Summative* evaluations, in contrast, gauge the success of mature, already-complete educational interventions.

In the following few paragraphs, I'll describe how formative assessment functions, and how teachers (and students, too) use it. You'll easily recognize the ends-means structure at work. The process begins with a teacher identifying a *target curricular aim*—otherwise known as a learning outcome that students are supposed to master. Typically, this sought-for curricular aim will be a challenging cognitive skill of some sort (such as being able to formulate hypothesis-testing research strategies) to be mastered during an instructional unit that consumes a serious chunk of teaching time (typically, a few weeks up to a full semester). Any kind of curricular ends could be pursued through formative assessment; the reason they are usually high-level cognitive skills is that implementing the formative assessment process takes a serious level of teacher effort. Why spend it in pursuit of a trifling curricular aim?

Next, the teacher creates an end-of-unit test to measure students' mastery of the unit's aim—and this next step is essential—then devises a *learning progression* to identify the most important *building blocks* thought to lead to that mastery. These are the *cognitive subskills* or *bodies of enabling knowledge* that students must master on their way to mastering the unit's target curricular aim. Then, the teacher creates an assessment to determine students' mastery of *each* building block. These assessments need not be formal paper-and-pencil tests, but they can be.

With the prep complete, the unit can begin. As it proceeds, the teacher administers the appropriate building-block assessment near the close of the instructional activities aimed at each building block. Based on students' test performances, the teacher either makes no adjustments in instruction or, in the instructional time still available, makes an instructional adjustment aimed at improving students' learning outcome. This might mean trying a different technique or speeding up or slowing the pace of instruction for some students or all students. It might mean introducing a different hook to increase engagement with the topic or going back to readdress a certain skill component, a certain text, or a certain understanding. The particular adjustments a teacher makes will be a judgment call, informed by the assessment evidence. (To be candid, figuring out better ways to teach something when your first attempt at teaching it seems to have flopped is one of the hardest tasks in formative assessment. Nonetheless, coming up with alternative means is often required.) This, in a walnut shell, is what a teacher does during the formative assessment process.

Students have a role to play, too. While teachers are using the assessment-elicited evidence to figure out if and how and to adjust their instructional practices, students can use it to evaluate the effectiveness of their learning tactics and decide whether to adjust how they are trying to master a particular building block in the learning progression. Many teachers hope to foster a collection of self-monitoring and self-adapting students, and regular deployment of formative assessment over time surely helps develop these capacities. Skillful teachers can offer help along the way by providing students who need "what else might work" ideas with an array of options for adjusting their learning tactics. Such suggestions might range from new study procedures and atypical practice drills to different ways of approaching and interacting with the unit's content by relying on peer study groups.

Based on my own interactions with North American educators and foreign educators who are interested in formative assessment, I have concluded that whereas U.S. educators usually focus on the ways that formative assessment can be used to improve *teachers'* instructional efforts, in many other nations, especially in Europe and Australasia, formative assessment proponents are most interested in how it can empower *students* to become self-governing learners.

Learning Progressions: Frameworks for Fine Teaching

Learning progressions function as the organizational structures for implementing the formative assessment process. Accordingly, we should take a closer look at them, reviewing what learning progressions are and then considering a few choices teachers have in their creation and implementation.

A learning progression is a sequenced set of subskills and bodies of enabling knowledge its creator believes students must master en route to mastering a more remote curricular aim. I typically refer to this more remote curricular aim as the *target curricular aim* and the must-be-mastered subskills and bodies of enabling knowledge as the learning progression's *building blocks*. As a side note, I recommend anyone who is working with colleagues to generate learning progressions agree at the outset on the terminology that will be used. It will save confusion later.

Because there's often a fair amount of work associated with planning and implementing the formative assessment process, it's best reserved for big-deal outcomes—*challenging* cognitive skills, such the ability to plan and deliver an informational speech or to write a persuasive essay. Therefore, the first step in writing a learning progression for formative assessment is confirming that the target curricular aim is suitably signif-icant to make the ensuing effort worthwhile. One way to approach this question is to consider how much instructional time the mastery of this curricular aim will require. If the answer is "several weeks," "an entire school term," or "the whole academic year," chances are that this curric-ular aim is worth assessing formatively and worth mapping as a learning progression.

Figure 6.2 presents a simple graphic depiction of a learning progres-sion intended to cover a three-week instructional unit. Note that one of the three building blocks consists of a body of enabling knowledge and that the other two building blocks are subskills. The number of lessons needed for each building block has been estimated in a time line below the three building blocks.

FIGURE 6.2 | A Learning Progress with Lesson Number Estimates

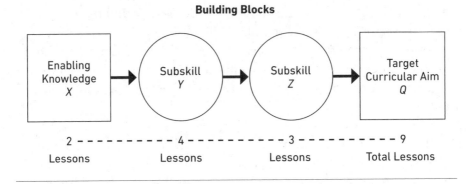

If this point is not already clear, learning progressions are not generated in secret learning-progression factories run by educators who are addicted to linearity. Teachers build learning progressions. Teachers figure out what are the *most significant* curricular aims they want their students to accomplish, then decide which of those aims they intend to pursue by employing the formative assessment process. Next, teachers try to generate a serviceable learning progression for instructionally pursuing each aim. The essential requirements for building a learning progression involve identifying the building blocks that students *must* master if they're going to succeed in mastering the target curricular aim.

How many building blocks is the right number of building blocks? Answers vary. I believe teachers must be wary of identifying too many; remember, each building block must be assessed to generate evidence that will help determine if instructional or learning approaches require adjustment. Too much testing, even in pursuit of worthy curricular aims, is still, by definition, *too much testing*. You might sustain it for a while, but you won't like it over the long haul, and neither will your students.

A good friend of mine, Margaret Heritage, has done a lot of impeccable thinking and writing about formative assessment and learning progressions. She and I have had some healthy squabbles about the nature of the latter. Margaret would prefer that learning progressions focus on students' attainment of super-major curricular outcomes such as a field's "big ideas" and last for an instructional period of up to several years (Heritage, 2010). I prefer learning progressions that deal with important but less grand curricular targets that can be addressable instructionally in weeks or months. Recently, Margaret has called for states to supply inter-grade-level progressions of curricular aims in support of formative assessment (Andrade & Heritage, 2018). This makes sense to me. She would like to see learning progressions be based on scientific research supporting the sequence of a learning progression's building blocks. I, however, am happy to rely on teachers' professional judgment, and that means the best building-block sequences that subject-expert classroom teachers can devise analytically.

She may be right; so too might I. Perhaps we both are. What's important to recognize is that, much as there's no designated source for learning progressions, there is no single profession-sanctioned model for building and using them. Despite this, learning progressions are the ideal framework for effective formative assessment, because they represent a reasonable way for teachers to map out and monitor the success of their instructional means as they work toward a clearly identified learning end.

Why Isn't Formative Assessment More Prevalent?

We now turn to a vexing problem facing today's educators, and it jumps out at us from the second and third words in the Formative Assessment Understanding. Those two words are "currently underused."

There exists an enormously effective way of helping students learn better, an approach that has been authenticated by heaps of research evidence, yet it is not used widely by today's teachers. Again, formative assessment is a *proven* method of enhancing students' learning, but it is not being used in the majority of U.S. classrooms. *How can this be?* If I sound somewhat baffled, it is because I am somewhat baffled.

I have thought long and hard about the current underuse of formative assessment, yet I have little more to offer than a handful of speculations. Here are a few of those conjectures.

When American educators, attempting to dodge the slings and arrows of NCLB, first began exploring formative assessment—some assessment-rooted instructional strategy that two British researchers had asserted could boost students' scores on accountability tests—few written explanations of how to make formative assessment function were available. I concluded that the absence of readily accessible written materials was holding back the more expansive usage of formative assessment.

Accordingly, swathed in pure pluck, I wrote an explanatory book about formative assessment for ASCD (Popham, 2008). Because it was chosen to be an ASCD Member Book, it reached a substantial number of American educators and helped raise the profile of formative assessment—at least a bit. The actual increase in teachers' *usage* of formative assessment, however, was quite modest. Today, there are numerous first-rate explanatory books about the formative assessment process, many written by colleagues whom I am fortunate enough to call friends. I can particularly recommend books by Larry Ainsworth (2015), Heidi Andrade and Margaret Heritage (2018), Susan Brookhart (2013), Margaret Heritage (2010), Rick Stiggins and Jan Chappuis (2017), and Dylan Wiliam (2011). And even with all these different, well-written views on how to make formative assessment flourish, the process is still underused. It is advocated in print and during staff meetings, but it's still rarely seen in U.S. classrooms.

My current working hypothesis as to why? *I think many teachers, with good reason, regard formative assessment as simply too much trouble.* It's piqued the interest of many, and many have set out adopt it, but they have done so in a way that soon causes them to abandon the approach altogether. Formative assessment, done properly, is a carefully planned process whose implementation takes time—and time to spare is not a luxury that many teachers enjoy.

Here's an example of how daily reality can derail the best formative assessment intentions. Say a teacher identifies 10 genuinely significant curricular outcomes that students need to accomplish by the end of the school year. Perhaps these outcomes are assessed on the state's annual accountability tests, and perhaps they aren't. Then the teacher sets out to apply the formative assessment process to promote students' mastery of all 10 of these targets. That's 10 learning progressions to generate. For each of these 10 learning progressions, there are assessments to select or create for each building block. And this soon works out to be an exponential number of assessment results to interpret and instructional adjustments to devise and implement. Pulling all this off and retaining one's sanity often constitutes a verifiable instructional miracle.

My advice boils down to this: be liberal in your advocacy of formative assessment and conservative in your practice of it. I would rather have a teacher use formative assessment only once or twice during a school year and *continue to use it* than to try to use formative assessment all the time and then abandon it entirely after a year or two because the work is too onerous. It is much more sensible to adopt an ever-so-incremental, time-conscious implementation strategy than to charge headlong into applying formative assessment during every lesson.

In the same way that I'd like to see teachers use formative assessment judiciously but consistently, I'd also rather see teachers *begin* their use of formative assessment to inform only *their* instructional decisions rather than leap in and try to use both teacher-focused *and* student-focused implementations of formative assessment simultaneously. If teachers recognize the dividends of applying ends-means thinking to their own teaching, they can thereafter sprinkle some of those dividends on their classes in the form of student-managed formative assessment.

Most of the writers I've cited in this chapter have offered their own advice on how best to make formative assessment succeed. I encourage you to explore these, and I believe that as long as those recommended approaches represent some serious incarnation of an ends-means instructional strategy, those approaches will work...if you actually use them and *keep using them*. As Black and Wiliam assert, "significant gains can be achieved by many different routes, and initiatives here are not likely to fail through neglect of delicate and subtle features" (1998a, p. 61). Formative assessment is so robust that it can be used gingerly and *still* be enormously effective.

The Understanding's Application

Here is an opportunity to get chummy with the Formative Assessment Understanding through a fictitious decision-requiring situation calling for you to supply an earnest response.

Please assume that you are a former high school history teacher who has just been elected to serve a three-year term on your district school board. At your very first meeting, you and the other eight members of the board must reach a final decision regarding an issue that has been debated during several previous meetings. A decision must be made regarding whether to formally purchase a commercially distributed set of "benchmark tests" at grades 3 through 8 for the district's elementary and middle schools. The tests are available in both mathematics and English language arts. Although the publisher describes these assessments as "benchmark" tests, some district educators also call them "interim" tests.

The board members who support the purchase argue that acquisition of these benchmark tests will profoundly encourage the district's teachers in grades 3 through 8 to implement the formative assessment process in their own classrooms. These board members point out that the positive learning impact of the formative assessment process has been amply supported by carefully controlled research studies here and abroad. These benchmark tests, they point out, can be used to gather performance data as students work toward the outcomes described in the grade-level standards. If teachers have these measurement tools at their disposal, they'll be more likely to use formative assessment, an instructional strategy that has been shown to benefit students' learning.

The curricular outcomes targeted in the interim tests match those that will assessed by the state's annual accountability tests. There are three test forms for each grade level (grades 3–8) and approximately 30 items per test form. Each test takes about 40 minutes to complete and can be administered via computer or with traditional paper-and-pencil means. The tests' publisher will supply immediate scoring of computer-administered tests and next-day scoring of students' responses submitted on scannable answer sheets. District administrators appear to favor the computer-based administration and scoring approach.

State officials have identified approximately a dozen curricular goals per grade level in both mathematics and English language arts, and each grade level's benchmark tests have been split up so that every test measures approximately one-third of that grade's state goals. This means about four curricular goals are to be assessed in each benchmark test. The publisher recommends the tests be administered approximately three times during the school year (using a different form each time). The testing window—that is, the time periods during which the tests are to be administered—would be determined by the district.

Because your board's purchase of these benchmark tests would constitute one of its largest financial outlays in recent years, the decision has received considerable attention from local media. The vote is fast approaching, and your fellow board members are deep in discussion of the pros and cons. What will your vote be? And why?

....

JIM'S DECISION

If I were a new board member, I would be careful not to come on too strongly, for novice board members ought to know their place. Yet, after circling for a while and concurring with the yearnings of some board members for teachers' greater reliance on the formative assessment process, I would ultimately urge rejection of the proposal to purchase the new benchmark tests.

Here's how I would try to make my points clearly—yet meekly—as befits my newcomer's position. Even though the chief rationale for purchasing the new interim tests is that their acquisition will stimulate greater use of formative assessment, there is no evidence—quantitative or anecdotal—suggesting that the availability of interim tests does any such thing. Actually, in settings where teachers must administer the sorts of interim tests described here, informal reports suggest that obligatory interim-test use actually decreases teachers' use of formative assessment.

Next, we need to think about what it means that the interim tests would be administered up to three times per year. In one way, this sounds positive—there's no plan to weigh teachers down with too-frequent required testing. But remember that, collectively, these interim tests are designed to sample a total of 24 curricular outcomes at each grade level—a dozen ELA outcomes and a dozen math ones. By necessity, each test would need to measure students' mastery of four ELA or math state-approved curricular outcomes at the same time. The only way to do that in a 40-minute test is through extremely skimpy sampling—the kind that does not support accurate interpretations of students' mastery with respect to instructionally addressable skills and bodies of knowledge. Consider, too, that teachers would need to match the timing of their instructional emphases to the timing of the test administrations. It will often be the case that teachers' instructional progress will not mesh optimally with the district-decreed testing windows. Through this lens, three times a year is far too infrequent to support the formative assessment process—even if the items that appeared on the test happened to align with the building blocks the teachers were addressing in class.

While there is a hoard of empirical evidence supporting the instructional dividends of formative assessment, this kind of testing-teaching mistiming inevitable with mandated interim tests may explain the absence of research evidence supporting any serious instructional payoffs linked to interim tests.

As a fledgling board member, I would applaud my more experienced colleagues' support of formative assessment, but I'd urge them, with newcomer deference, to pass on purchasing the new interim tests. I would most likely recommend instead adoption of a hefty professional-development strategy for the district whereby teachers could learn not only how to generate learning progressions but also how to craft tests capable of gauging students' evolving mastery of the building blocks needed to master target curricular aims.

For the Truly Time-Pressed

Here's another look at this chapter's component of assessment literacy:

The Formative Assessment Understanding

Although currently underused, formative assessment
is a remarkable, research-ratified process in which teachers
and students use classroom assessments to make needed adjustments
that can dramatically improve students' learning.

* * * * *

The most salient components of this understanding are these:

1. Formative assessment's effectiveness is backed up by bundles of supportive research evidence.
2. Formative assessment is a process employed by teachers and sometimes students to adjust what they are doing in order to achieve important curricular goals.
3. Formative assessment is used far less frequently than it ought to be.

Is this three-element understanding one of the six most important things that today's educators need to understand about assessment? As you have certainly inferred by now, I think it is. Getting more educators to grasp the what, the why, and the various hows of formative assessment so that they and their students will realize its enormous benefits represents my identified end. The Formative Assessment Understanding, and all you've just read about it, are my means. I hope that this application of ends-means advocacy will work on you.

7 MEASURING AFFECT

Getting a Fix on Behavioral Changes

Ben Bloom started it.

If you're looking to give credit or cast blame for educators' attempts to influence students' attitudes, interests, and values, please aim your applause or condemnation at the late Benjamin S. Bloom, a University of Chicago professor who, along with a flock of colleagues, published the *Taxonomy of Educational Objectives* (Bloom, Engelhart, Furst, Hill, & Krathwohl, 1956) more than 60 years ago. As Bloom himself once told me during an airport shuttlebus ride, this was a book that attracted almost *zero* interest for several years after its publication. But to his surprise and that of his coauthors, sales of the *Taxonomy* took off seriously in the early 1960s. Soon, it became a top-of-the-charts educational bestseller and remained so for years.

The U.S. government played a role in the popularity of Bloom's taxonomy. According to guidelines spelled out for implementing the Elementary and Secondary Education Act of 1965, American educators were urged to explicate their instructional intentions far more crisply than in years past. Gunky, generally stated curricular objectives like "Students will grasp the importance of historical events" were no longer sufficient. Teachers were told by federal authorities that they needed to clarify their instructional intentions for any federally supported educational endeavors. They needed to plan their lessons in a way that would promote students' mastery of *behavioral objectives*, so called because these objectives would identify the measurable behaviors students would be able to display after successful instruction.

Three Flavors of Educational Goals

I suspect one reason Bloom and company's *Taxonomy of Educational Objectives* struck a chord was because it divided these objectives into three categories—*cognitive, affective*, and *psychomotor*—thus offering educators a more expansive vocabulary for conceptualizing the kinds of educational ends they might promote.

Cognitive educational objectives call for students to acquire *knowledge* or *skills*. More specifically, students must master a body of knowledge (such as having memorized our most widely used punctuation and capitalization conventions) or master an intellectual skill (such as being able to formulate and implement hypothesis-testing scientific experiments). For centuries, the pursuit of cognitive goals has been the predominant preoccupation of our schools.

Affective educational objectives describe instructional outcomes dealing with students' noncognitive dispositions, more specifically, their attitudes, interests, or values. Because this chapter centers on affective assessment, we'll soon be looking somewhat more deeply into what's meant by attitudes, interests, and values. But, in looking back to see when it was that many American educators began displaying any sort of interest in the affective outcomes of education, the relevant DNA trail leads us right back to Bloom's taxonomy.

Finally, *psychomotor* objectives deal with students' attainment of small-muscle physical skills, such as computer keyboarding, or large-muscle physical skills, such as pole vaulting. Although substantial attention has been given to the nature of cognitive outcomes and, to a lesser extent, to affective outcomes, psychomotor objectives remain the neglected third wheel of educational outcomes. This inattention likely springs from the fact that relatively few teachers are charged with the promotion of students' psychomotor achievements.

Throughout the 1960s and 1970s, ends-focused behavioral objectives became a widely endorsed way for teachers to state the instructional aspirations that they had for their students. Both Bloom's taxonomy and the terminology in that 1956 publication are still taught in schools of education as guideposts for lesson planning.

Affect Ascending

Perhaps you're wondering why I'm bringing up a categorization of educational aims, something that has been around for more than six decades? It's an appropriate question, and here's my response: I do so in a blatant attempt to rebalance today's curricular aspirations.

Although the *Taxonomy of Educational Objectives* discussed cognitive, affective, and psychomotor educational objectives, it dealt almost exclusively with the cognitive ones, as the book's subtitle—*Handbook I: Cognitive Domain*—makes clear. Promoting students' mastery of knowledge and skills was where educators' attention was centered back in those days, and where it has largely remained. Yet, when contrasting the *educational importance* of promoting cognitive, affective, and psychomotor changes in students, you'll find a fair number of educators—including the affable author of this book—who think that affective outcomes are wildly underrated. Let's talk about why.

How a student feels, what he or she values, and what he or she is interested in powerfully *dispose* the student to act in particular ways—both in the immediate future and well into the distant one. Few educators would disagree with this commonsense conclusion. If asked to choose between (a) promoting students' positive attitudes toward mathematics *or* (b) increasing those same students' mastery of key cognitive skills in math, I'd opt for positive attitude promotion. Yes, working to increase students' mastery of key cognitive skills would likely have an immediate benefit, but promoting the affective goal of creating a math-positive attitude is a canny long-term investment that will ultimately lead more students to master mathematics. It's because of the impact that students' current dispositions will have on their future *behavior* that educators need to address and, yes, *assess*, affect.

Seeking Evidence of Dispositions

As Figure 7.1 illustrates, students' current affective status provides us with a powerful predictor of how those students are apt to behave in the future. Think of how young students who like their teacher and *feel liked* by that teacher will be inclined to conduct themselves in class. Think of how students who enjoy volitional, nonrequired reading are more likely to carry this disposition forward through their schooling into adulthood. Think of how students who enjoy scientific exploration and experimentation, tinkering and problem solving, will be more likely to pursue and engage in coursework related to these interests and more likely to enter professions where they can continue doing the sort of work they love. Now think of students who hate mathematics, or hate their teacher, or hate school in general. Consider the impact these dispositions will have on their current learning, future schooling, and careers.

FIGURE 7.1 | Students' Current Affective Status and Their Future Behavior

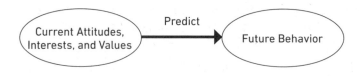

The time-bending logic here is that educators ought to assess affect because doing so gives them a reasonably accurate fix on students' predicted future conduct and, thus, informs the actions they might take to influence what students' actual future conduct will be.

Three Flavors of Student Affect

When we talk about affect in school settings, what exactly are we talking about? These are the realms of motivation and engagement—those elusive, noncognitive factors that have a profound effect on individual learning. I've broken affect down into three categories for easier scrutiny: *attitudes, interests,* and *values.*

Attitudes

My dictionary describes an attitude as a "settled way of thinking or feeling about a person or thing." That seems about right to me. Attitudes are complex emotions that can be unpacked in extended paragraphs but are often best summed up in simple, understandable shorthand: positive or negative, appropriate or inappropriate.

A student's attitude about people or things influences the way that a student responds to those people or things. For example, if a student has a positive, respectful attitude toward classmates who have a different racial background, that student is more likely to engage in positive, respectful behaviors toward those classmates. This reverse is also true: negative, disrespectful attitudes about such classmates are more likely to result in negative, disrespectful behaviors. Shifting the example to an academic one, just think of the disparate behaviors likely to result from a positive, open attitude toward mathematics learning ("It's fun! It's like exploring!") and a negative, defeatist one ("It's awful; it's too hard; I'll never get it!"). Figure 7.1 provides a tidy summary of this attitude effect.

Angela Duckworth's (2016) advocacy of grit as an important component of success is part of this conversation. *Grit* is generally defined as an individual's resiliency and ability to summon the motivation to achieve goals. It's increasingly recognized as a noncognitive variable that can powerfully influence students' achievement. Empirical research attesting to the significant role that student *effort* plays in improving *achievement* provides backup (Hattie & Yates, 2014). As an attitudinal variable of significance, grit fuels perseverance that can trigger the levels of effort students must expend to reach their goals.

Interests

Students' *interests* are those things that attract them, involve them, and engage their emotions or their intellect. Savvy educators know that motivation to learn increases when students feel a connection to or passion for the content (Piaget, 1978; Wolfe, 2010), and they try to design instruction that not only capitalizes on the interests their students have but also builds interest in curriculum content. As kids traverse the education trail from kindergarten through 12th grade, there are oodles of entities that might draw their interest and, thus, serve as potential points of instructional leverage. Accordingly, the *really* savvy educators undertake some thoughtful prioritizing and work to isolate, then nurture, a modest set of the *most* influential interests that will pay the most desirable dividends over time.

Values

My favorite abbreviated definition of *values*, the third member of our affective dimension triumvirate, is someone's "judgments about what is important in life."

As children grow up, gain familiarity with their society's culture, and receive input and guidance from parents, guardians, and peers, they have many opportunities to arrive at their own judgments about what is important in life. I believe a nation's schools can play a powerful role in shaping the emerging values of the children they are educating. But I also know when it comes to promoting the acquisition of values, educators must proceed with wisdom and caution, and this means concentrating on big, noncontroversial values that are endorsed by darn near everyone. Yes, there are still important, near-universally approved values that can be defensively promoted—things like honesty, integrity, justice, and kindness.

Even in schools where the emphasis on cognitive curricular outcomes is the heaviest, most educators still have at least a bit of instructional latitude to foster students' acquisition of a few affective outcomes. Given the positive impact that affective dispositions can have on students' behaviors in school and beyond, I urge you to consider setting and pursuing at least a few disposition-determining affective aims. If you accept this invitation, you'll soon see where—and why—assessment of affect must enter the scene. Accordingly, it is time to formally present this chapter's contribution to assessment literacy:

The Affective Assessment Understanding

Because affective dispositions acquired in school can have a profound influence on students' success, both during and following school, students' affect should be assessed regularly, using anonymously completed self-report inventories.

* * * * *

As you can see, the first part of this chapter's Affective Assessment Understanding reiterates my rah-rah support for the virtues of affective assessment. The advocacy continues thereafter, with a call for regular affective assessment and guidance for how to go about it.

Understanding the Understanding

Having read this much of my thinly masked attempt to applaud the glories of affective assessment, you've probably already made up your mind about the merits of measuring students' affect. As with many curricular calls, whether to pursue particular affective aims will always boil down to a teacher's judgment. But those judgments should not be made without accepting the sometimes-vexing reality that choosing to pursue affective outcomes essentially obliges a teacher to *measure* whether those outcomes are attained. Absent such measurement, the advocacy of affective outcomes usually turns out to be talk—and often empty talk at that.

There are special complications associated with assessing students' attitudes, interests, and values. No teacher should try to influence aspects of students' affect without first grasping what sort of assessing it will involve.

The Allure of Anonymity

There's a mostly unspoken deal between educators and students that we can trace to our earliest days of school, that time when primary teachers urge tiny boys and girls at tiny desks to "Do your best!"

The calculus of assessment assumes that test-takers will always try to do their best—perform as well as they can on whatever test they've been told to complete. This assumption holds true whether the students are providing paper-and-pencil responses to a multiple-choice test, writing expository essays, completing project work, or taking basketball shots from the free throw line. Educators trust that students are exerting sincere effort to achieve a designated outcome or, at least, to earn a good score.

The assessment of affect calls for a decidedly different measurement strategy and an alternative score interpretation approach. When we assess students' affect, we are trying to get a reasonably accurate fix on students' attitudes, interests, or values, and the evidence we rely on to do so are the responses that the students supply. But no optimal answer or skill demonstration is expected. In a sense, this "freedom to fool us" requires substantial shifts in the ways we design affective assessment instruments and how we go about interpreting students' responses.

It is, of course, theoretically possible to collect sophisticated physical or neurological evidence that's indicative of the degree to which students possess specific affective dispositions. But even with the necessary technology, this would be prohibitively expensive and time-consuming. Imagine getting small and sometimes-squirmy children wired up with suitable electronic patches and galvanic skin monitors... that's no easy task. From a practicability perspective, it makes much more sense to simply *ask* students about their attitudes, interests, or values. Therefore, the bulk of today's affective assessment instruments are *self-report inventories*. Lorin Anderson and Sid Bourke (2000) present a persuasive case for using self-report inventories to assess student affect. We'll dig into the details of these assessment instruments in just a bit, but it's important to talk about a catch that can skew the validity of the inferences we draw from them.

Students, like just about all human beings, want others to think well of them. Thus, for instance, when we ask students to indicate how confident they are in their ability to deliver an oral report to their classmates, some, knowing confidence to be a desirable trait, will assert that they possess far more confidence than they actually do. The operative phenomenon here is called *social desirability*, which is the well-established tendency of individuals to inflate their responses on self-report inventories to present themselves in a way that will garner the approval of others.

The best way to circumvent the response distortion that social desirability inclinations trigger is to build affective assessments that provide genuine *anonymity*. We are *not* looking for students to respond *optimally,* as we are when we're measuring their mastery of cognitive objectives; we want students to respond *honestly*.

Building affective assessments without a space for a student's name is the best way to get honest responses, but it's not a foolproof one. Some students are still likely to respond in a way that indicates more positivity than they really feel, believing that it will be better if their teacher sees the sorts of responses most teachers seem to want. For example, in a classroom where the teacher has been emphasizing the importance of working hard to complete homework, most students will realize that the teacher hopes their anonymous self-report inventories will support the merits of working hard to complete homework. On the other hand, there will usually be students who conversely use the cloak of anonymity to lob responses that are disingenuously negative. Maybe they are looking to "even the score" with a teacher for a perceived offense; maybe they are expressing a deeper sense of disillusionment. To some extent, these too-positive and too-negative responses tend to cancel each other out—but not perfectly. And it is such imperfect matches that lead us to the sorts of inferences we can cautiously but legitimately draw from students' responses to anonymously completed self-report inventories. Let's look at those inferences now.

Group-Focused Inferences Only

It would be terrific if the use of anonymous self-report inventories would allow us to draw reasonably accurate affective inferences about individual students. *But they don't, and we can't.* Obviously, if students are completing self-report inventories *anonymously*, as they must if we want honest responses, there is simply no way to tie any interpretations about affective status to a particular student. Anonymity, after all, means anonymity. However, it *is* possible to use responses to self-report inventories to arrive at defensible *group-focused inferences* about students' affect, and to take affect-focused instructional actions based on such inferences.

Please don't shortchange the educational usefulness of group-focused inferences. If a 3rd grade teacher discovers, via anonymous self-report inventories, that her entire class of 3rd graders is positive about its free-time reading activities, then the teacher can take this evidence into consideration when planning for similar reading-related activities in the future. In contrast, if more students than not react negatively to having free time for reading, the teacher will be well-served to dig into why this is so. Should the selection of reading material be changed to align better with student skills or interests? Is she providing enough reading support? What other factors might be limiting her students' enjoyment of free-reading time? Group-focused inferences about affect can make an enormous difference in the ways teachers end up teaching their students and in the ways students experience learning.

Constructing Affective Self-Report Inventories

The construction of affectively focused self-report inventories is neither rocket science nor fools' play. If you want to learn more about how to gin up some serviceable affective self-report inventories, a quick dash to an online search engine will supply you with a bevy of useful resources for building and buffing up such inventories. I can recommend, with blatant partiality, the advice that's supplied in a scintillating chapter on affective assessment in an oft-revised book of mine (Popham, 2017a). Truly, just a bit of background reading about the basics of affective assessment will set you up to create serviceable self-report inventories that, when administered anonymously, can yield actionable inferences about a student group's affective status.

Most affective self-report inventories mimic the measurement model provided way, way back—more than three-quarters of a century ago—by Rensis Likert (1932). A Likert-like inventory asks respondents to indicate the degree to which they agree or disagree with a series of statements related to a specific topic or topics. For example, a Likert-like inventory might contain the statement "I really enjoy watching news programs on television," followed by these possible responses:

Strongly Agree, Agree, Not Sure, Disagree, or *Strongly Disagree.* Or you might see response options *True for me* or *Not true for me.* Statements can be phrased positively, as the example just shown, or negatively (for example, "I do not enjoy watching news programs on television").

As mentioned, there is plenty of guidance available on how to write strong self-report inventories, but I'll highlight just one key thing I've learned by whomping up many such inventories. Because the purpose of these inventories is to help a teacher differentiate among students' affect, the statements cannot be phrased in too absolute a way. For example, you wouldn't want to try to assess students' attitude toward school with a statement like "I would rather eat gravel than miss a day of school." No one likes school *that* much! A statement phrased like this would generate a lot of *Disagree* and *Strongly Disagree* responses, even from students who value attendance and usually look forward to coming to school. When the statements in an affective self-report inventory are structured to be very positive or very negative, they often won't elicit the sorts of varied responses needed to arrive at valid, group-focused inferences about students' differing degrees of attitudes, interests, or values.

Likert's original inventories focused exclusively on a single affective dimension, meaning all the statements in a 10- to 20-statement inventory were designed to gather data about the same subject (say, students' attitudes toward mandatory military service). This approach certainly provides a comprehensive data set, but creating and administering lengthy "original version" Likert inventories can take a ton of time. It's far more common today, and more practical, to devote two to four statements to a single affective dimension. So, for example, a teacher might create a six-statement inventory focused on three affective variables and include one positively stated and one negatively stated statement for each variable. Or a teacher might create an eight-item inventory focused on only two affective variables and write four statements per variable—split between positive and negative statements. These "Likert-like" self-report inventories allow teachers to tap into students' reactions to a number of affective variables, and to do so efficiently without intruding on too much instructional time.

Most teachers who employ affective inventories with their classes tend to administer such inventories on more than one occasion during the school year. This permits teachers to discern if there are any meaningful changes taking place in the affective dispositions of their students. Such changes, of course, can often trigger a need for suitable action on the part of a teacher.

A Just-for-You Affective Inventory

There's been so much attention given in this chapter to the use of affectively focused self-report inventories that I thought it might be useful to show you an example of one that I churned out just for this book. No, it has not been piloted with 5,000 students, revised myriad times, or been the recipient of a major award from a prestigious measurement society. Its only mission is to provide an illustration of what a teacher who decided to create an affective self-report inventory might turn out. This inventory, shown in Figure 7.2, is written for students in grades 4 through 6 and addresses several different aspects "self-managed learning." Please take a look at it.

The first thing I'd like to point out is that this inventory's directions includes an underscored admonition that students are to submit their completed inventories anonymously, but it does so without using the word *anonymously*. Although anonymity is crucial in the measurement of students' affect, it's important to remember to pitch all aspects of a self-report inventory to the students who will be using it. The term *anonymity* might be a little much for 4th, 5th, and 6th graders.

Second, let's identify the distinctive elements of self-managed learning that this 10-item inventory treats:

- Items 1 and 6 try to get at students' sentiments regarding the importance of knowing in advance what they are expected to learn;
- Items 2 and 7 focus on the importance of judging one's ongoing work;
- Items 3 and 8 target feelings about the significance of school success;
- Items 4 and 9 deal with the perceived need to have evidence of one's overall success; and
- Items 5 and 10 attempt to get at a student's sense of being able to employ optional approaches to learning.

This kind of item pairing helps to make the inventory *actionable*. Because the paired items deal with a single focus, we can cautiously think of those item-pair responses as "subscale scores." Agreement with one statement of that pair earns a positive score; disagreement with the

FIGURE 7.2 | An Illustrative Affective Inventory

A SELF-MANAGED LEARNING INVENTORY

Directions: *Please indicate whether you agree or disagree with each of the following 10 statements about school. Some statements are positive; some are negative. There are no right or wrong answers; just answer honestly. Do not write your name on the inventory or make any written comments on it. Only make X marks, one for each statement.*

Here is a sample: Response (one per statement)

	Agree	**Disagree**	**Not Sure**
I like watching movies.	☒	❏	❏

When you are finished, a classmate will collect your inventory and put it in an envelope with the other inventories collected. Thanks for your help and your honesty.

Response (one per statement)

	Agree	**Disagree**	**Not Sure**
1. I always like to know what I am supposed to learn before I try to learn it.	❏	❏	❏
2. While I am doing work, it's not that important to me to be able to judge how good it is.	❏	❏	❏
3. Overall, I like to be successful in class and learn what I am expected to learn.	❏	❏	❏
4. I don't need ways to judge how successful my learning is.	❏	❏	❏
5. If the way I'm trying to learn something isn't working, I try alternative methods.	❏	❏	❏
6. Much of the time, it doesn't matter to me if I know in advance what I'm expected to learn.	❏	❏	❏
7. While I am doing my work, I always want to be able to track how well I'm doing.	❏	❏	❏
8. Sometimes it's not very important to me if I am successful in school.	❏	❏	❏
9. I like being able to know how well I have learned everything taught in class.	❏	❏	❏
10. If the way I try to learn something does not work, I'd rather ask for help than figure out another way on my own.	❏	❏	❏

other statement of that pair earns a positive score. A responding student gets two bites out of the apple.

To illustrate, let's say that we have decided to award a score of two points to each response that agrees with a statement expressing a preference for self-managed learning, and a score of zero for each response that disagrees. All *Not Sure* responses receive a score of one point. With these scoring rules, the most positive overall score a student could earn would be 20 points, indicating agreement with all statements consistent with a self-managed learning stance and disagreement with all statements inconsistent with a self-managed learning stance. Of course, we could also take a more granular look at the five individual components and calculate scores up to 4 for each pair of items.

Remember, the goal is to make score-based interpretations for an entire *group* of students.

Consider, for example, Ms. Clark, who teaches 5th grade. She is a strong proponent of self-managed learning and would like to see her 5th graders acquire increasingly positive attitudes toward self-managed learning during their time with her. She administers the Figure 7.2 inventory four times during the school year, once at its beginning, once at its end, and twice about three months apart in the middle of the school year.

Let's imagine that following one of her mid-year administrations of the inventory, Ms. Clark has calculated both a total 20-item score and 5 item-pair scores for her class. If she discovers that her students' responses to one item-pair (Items 2 and 8) are markedly lower than their other item-pair scores, she'd be right to infer that there may be work needed to foster attitudes consonant with the affective variable those items target (valuing the ability to judge the quality of one's day-to-day work).

Taking Action on Affect

This brings us to an important point. Teachers shouldn't be measuring their students' affect merely because it is "interesting." No, if Ms. Clark or you or any other educator is going to invest time and energy in measuring students' current receptiveness to self-guided learning, how confident they are in their ability to solve problems, how interested they are in scientific exploration, how much they value treating their peers with respect, or any other affective objective—these efforts ought to lead to *action*.

The first step is to examine the evidence and make what you believe to be a valid inference about students' overall status (e.g., their confidence is shaky, they are very enthusiastic about exploration, they don't seem to think that being respectful matters very much). The second step is to decide if you will attempt to instructionally address some or all of the sampled affective dimensions. This is a matter of judgment-based prioritization. The third step is to figure out *how* to go about influencing your chosen affective objectives through instruction.

As it turns out, the instructional techniques that research shows to be the most successful in altering students' affect are profoundly different from instructional procedures that research shows to be effective at promoting cognitive outcomes (Anderson & Bourke, 2000). If you are a teacher who wants to address affect, or if you supervise or lead such teachers, it's advisable to seek or provide meaningful guidance on the matter. Actionable affective inferences *unaccompanied* by knowledge of what actions teachers might take will surely engender frustration in many teachers.

To illustrate, one of the most powerful techniques educators use when shaping students' affect is *modeling*. When teachers are admired by their students, those teachers' views of the world are often emulated and adopted by their students. Little time need be expended, for example, in a teacher's subscribing to the importance of effort in promoting students' achievements, but students' adoption of a pro-effort stance can make a gigantic difference in the way some students will think about their own levels of effort. In the affective realm, whether the modeler is an esteemed teacher or an admired student, a short burst of suitable modeling can significantly shape students' affect. In sum, for relatively little effort, well-conceived affect-influencing activities based on students' properly measured affective status can often have a lasting effect on those students' lives.

I have been doing battle with affective assessment for almost a half-century, and I have the scars to prove it. Elsewhere (Popham, 2017a), I have described the most often employed instructional strategies for tackling the promotion of affective outcomes. Happily, via the mystical magic of the internet, one can find a fair number of suggestions regarding how best to influence students' affect. If you look over those instructional ploys, you'll find that they tend to be seriously different from our well-known, conventional ways of teaching children. If a collection of teachers in a school or district ever decided to get serious about altering students' affective dispositions, a rewarding, two-tactic strategy for them to conceptualize such an effort would be to focus on the *assessment* of and then the *influence* of students' affect.

This brief brush with the bolts and nuts of using self-report inventories was intended to underscore that the task is relatively easy to do, can generate some worthwhile measures of students' affect, and is a strong impetus to spend at least some instructional time promoting defensible affective factors. That which is measured is typically treasured. And attention to affect, more often than not, will be a good thing for students.

The Understanding's Application

Here is your final opportunity to apply a newly acquired assessment-related understandings to a somewhat life-like situation.

For this exercise, please imagine that your district has decided to institute a program of social and emotional learning (SEL). The curriculum that has already been adopted features a number of affective dimensions including enthusiasm for new learning, empathy for classmates, and anti-bullying sentiments. Teachers are encouraged to come up with their own SEL strategies after reviewing a series of potential strategies set forth on the district's website.

In this exercise, you are an omniscient observer at a high school. The faculty council has approved a SEL-linked initiative called "Getting Grit!" designed to help students increase their levels of effort, stick-to-itiveness, and pluckiness when tackling challenging schoolwork. In concert with a general grit-building approach that all teachers agree to adopt, which includes setting expectations for hard work, talking about the tools of grit, and debriefing after practice sessions carefully designed to introduce frustration, all teachers are to administer a 15-item, anonymous Likert-like self-report inventory three times—at the beginning of the school year, at midterm time, and at the end of the school year. The inventory takes 15 to 20 minutes to complete and is distributed on a set day and at a set time in all classrooms. Completed inventories are collected for subsequent analysis by members of the high school's student council. Results are distributed to the entire student body within two weeks.

Today is self-report inventory administration day, the last one of the year. You are focusing your omniscient attention on Mr. Jennings, a history teacher. Although other teachers in the district are employing very different approaches to grapple with social and emotional learning, Mr. Jennings relies heavily on the measurement of his student group's affect. At the appointed time, he distributes what the students have come to call "the Gritventory," emphasizing the need for students to write nothing on their inventories—no names or any means of identification. "Remember, we want to be sure your responses are truly untraceable," he says. "I know you'll do your best."

Mr. Jennings believes in the educational mission here—the promotion of resiliency and perseverance as skills that will serve his students well. When he administers the Gritventory to his history classes, the general response from his students is pretty much "grit-free," that is, his students obtain low scores on the anonymous self-report inventory. Those low scores incline Mr. Jennings to put some instructional attention into the promotion of greater grit among his students.

But he also suspects that shifts in his school's scores on the Gritventory are likely to be submitted to the district office and used to evaluate him and all the other teachers in his school. Accordingly, Mr. Jennings has devised several brief, grit-related classroom interventions that he thinks will enhance students' grit-leaning tendencies. He carried out these activities several weeks in advance of the mid-year and end-of-year administrations of the Gritventory. During these 20-minute "grit-getting" instructional sessions, he urged his students to do as well as they could in strengthening the grit with which they approach their school work, particularly their most difficult school work. For example, he has written a brief script for his students, and gets four of them to present this 10-minute sketch on the Payoffs of Perseverance to all his history classes. Mr. Jennings has also devised several other grit-specific lessons derived explicitly from certain items on the Gritventory. For instance, there is a lesson focused explicitly on the adverse consequences of giving up too early in an important quest.

This time, instead of asking you for a decision, I'd just like to know what observations you have about Mr. Jennings and his assessment of affect. For instance, how do you think he approached his challenge of altering students' grit? Were there any serious shortcomings in how he tackled this task instructionally?

....

JIM'S DECISION

Although I could use this space to make a substantial number of observations (author's privilege!), I'll keep it simple: the educators at this high school seem to be doing a reasonably good job of promoting the affective ends they're pursuing.

The one worry that I have relates to the impression Mr. Jennings may have promoted regarding how his students ought to respond to administrations of the Gritventory. If, at the beginning of the school year, he did anything to convey the impression that improvement in his classes' scores would be desirable, his students might very well have "gone low" on the initial administration of the Gritventory, then deliberately boosted their scores on subsequent administrations of these self-report inventories. Remember, most students can readily discern which direction of response is the "preferred" direction on self-report affective inventories.

And this possibility raises the more general issue of assessment validity. If a teacher's blatant or even subtle advocacy of the "right" way to respond to this self-report affective inventory influences how students' respond, any Gritventory-based inferences about students' level of grit are apt to be invalid and, therefore, the resultant grit-shaping activities ineffectual. When assessing students' affect, it's always important to give great attention to avoid advertising the sorts of responses sought.

....

For the Truly Time-Pressed

Let's take another look at this chapter's highlighted assessment understanding:

The Affective Assessment Understanding

Because affective dispositions acquired in school can have
a profound influence on students' success, both during and
following school, students' affect should be assessed regularly
using anonymously completed self-report inventories.

* * * * *

If a group of educators is committed to exploring what, if anything, can be done to improve students' affect, then those educators are off and running. By employing anonymous self-report inventories to ascertain a student *group's* affective dispositions, educators can readily decide whether to devote any instructional energy to the modification of such affect. In preparing to determine which instructional tactics to adopt, teachers will generally need to learn about the potential tactics deemed suitable for the modification of students' affect.

This concluding assessment-related understanding is pretty straightforward. It says that affect is important, that it ought to be measured routinely, and that this measurement should be carried out via anonymously completed self-report inventories.

But here's the nifty thing about affective assessment: a lot can be done with a little. Modest effort on the part of a teacher in students' affect can sometimes change the lives of students. I can recall with pleasure my first years in teaching when a smart move I made with a student turned around that student's school life for the better. Unfortunately, I can also recall doing truly dumb things that had an equally detrimental impact on the way certain students were functioning in school. The impact of affect on students' lives is often enormous. Its impact can be positive or negative. So, if you decide to move personally into the realm of students' affective modification, be sure to do so with at least rudimentary knowledge about the assessment and influence of students' attitudes, interests, and values. Affect is too important to mess up.

WRAPPING UP, REACHING OUT 8

This is the book's final chapter, and I would love to close out with some sort of spectacular special effect. Alas, my publisher specifically prohibited me from bundling the book with a set of celebratory fireworks, so I must move to Plan B.

And here it is. I have presented this concluding chapter in two readily distinguishable parts. The first is "Wrapping Up," in which I will briefly review the six fundamental understandings required for assessment literacy, sing your virtues for having acquired them, and remind you of all the good you can do now that you are assessment literate.

The second part of the chapter, "Reaching Out," is something to kickstart that do-gooding. It consists of four op-ed essays articulating your author's chief worries about the ways educational tests are being used in the United States today. Through the years, I've written many of these op-ed essays for publication in regional and national newspapers; these four I whomped up just for this book, which means I wrote these essays for you and for everyone else who might get the chance to read them.

Part I: Looking Back

This book's oft-announced mission was the promotion of assessment literacy via the presentation of six fundamental assessment understandings. The more educators we have who are assessment literate, the fewer muddled-headed mistakes we'll see made by educators who don't know their assessment onions.

When we truly understand the highest-priority notions about educational measurement and employ those understandings when making educational decisions, the beneficiaries of those evidence-informed decisions will be the children we educate. It is my firm conviction that if you comprehend and internalize the six assessment-related understandings presented in this book, your assessment literacy level will be sufficient to render your on-the-job decisions much sounder and more defensible. The beneficiaries of this enlightened decision making will be those you educate.

Huzzah for the Half-Dozen Understandings!

Gathered together in Figure 8.1 are the book's six assessment-related understandings.

"A little knowledge is a dangerous thing." If you've been alive for very long, you know how accurate this time-honored allegation is. People who own only the surface scrapings of a body of knowledge far too often believe they know more about it than they really do.

FIGURE 8.1 | The Fundamentals of Assessment Literacy

The Validity Understanding

Validity, the degree to which an evidence-based argument supports the accuracy of a test's interpretations for a proposed use of the test's results, is the necessary precursor to all educational assessment.

The Reliability Understanding

Assessment reliability, the consistency with which a test measures whatever it measures, is represented by three conceptually different kinds of evidence, and it should be reported for both test-taker groups and individual test-takers.

The Fairness Understanding

Fairness in educational testing is as important as validity and reliability in the creation and evaluation of tests, and it must be carefully documented—when practicable—with both judgmental and empirical evidence.

The Score Report Understanding

Because inferences about students are based on test-takers' score reports, users must demand that results be easily interpreted in accord with the test's intended use.

The Formative Assessment Understanding

Although currently underused, formative assessment is a remarkable, research-ratified process in which teachers and students use classroom assessments to make needed adjustments that can dramatically improve students' learning.

The Affective Assessment Understanding

Because affective dispositions acquired in school can have a profound influence on students' success, both during and following school, students' affect should be assessed regularly, using anonymously completed self-report inventories.

However, now that you grasp the book's six assessment-related understandings, your "little" knowledge about educational testing can diminish the most dangerous things being done to students because of someone else's shoddy grasp of educational assessment's basics. Your understanding of the *Joint Standards'* "big three" (validity, reliability, and test fairness) positions you well enough to raise questions about the suitability of tests being used, the inferences drawn from them, and the instructional policies and practices that flow from those inferences. You can, therefore, help to prevent the improper test use that contributes to poor educational decisions. You can steer your school, district, or state colleagues toward better test choices and better test-based decisions.

Understanding and championing the use of stronger score reports and of formative and affective assessment empowers you to put good test data to good use and, thereby, further student learning.

Additional Help Wanted: Assessment Translators

Back in Chapter 3's discussion of internal consistency reliability evidence, I pointed out how baffling the sophisticated technical reports that sometimes accompany high-stakes tests can be, even for educators who are assessment literate. Although you now understand the generalities of test mission, development, evaluation, and interpretation, you probably don't have the expertise necessary to personally carry out—or sometimes comprehend—the esoteric statistical analyses performed in connection with the evaluation of high-stakes tests.

And this is fine. You have other important work to do.

But what you and other assessment-literate educators could use from time to time is a *technical translator*. By that, I mean a *psychometrician*, an assessment specialist, usually graduate school–trained, who is not just capable of making sense of the complex reports meant to guide important educational decisions but also equipped to help assessment-literate educators like you navigate the puzzling minutiae of such reports.

To illustrate, I recently sat with state educational officials who were smack in the middle of deciding whether to switch from a set of state-constructed high school accountability tests to a pair of nationally distributed achievement tests. These officials had commissioned a state university to carry out a year-long investigation focused on comparing the current test with the new option. The university ultimately issued a remarkably technical report focused on the *Joint Standards'* "big three" features. But, because the evidence for validity, reliability, and test fairness was presented in such an opaque manner, few of the state officials involved could make much sense of the report. If they had only had a technical translator to help them interpret the report, they might have made better-informed decisions regarding the tests' relative merits.

Is the world full of technically savvy but plainspoken translators of technical testing reports? Regrettably, no. Therefore, it makes sense for us to reach out to graduate schools of education and urge them to create such a specialty. In 2017, I made an in-print pitch to the nation's school board members to lobby their local university's education offi-cials to prepare at least a modest number of such technical translators (Popham, 2017b). With the support of these specialists—assessment-knowledgeable educators who know that tests themselves aren't valid or invalid, that reliability comes to us in three different costumes, that bias can and should be hunted down and reduced, and that formative and affective assessment are powerful tools for improving learning—will be even better positioned to do good work.

Reaching Out

We've come to the how-else-you-might-help portion of the chapter.

I'll start with a few simple requests:

- If you run across an educational test that doesn't give all test-takers a fair chance to succeed, speak out.
- If you see that a high-stakes test is being used without proper vali-dation evidence to support the accuracy of its interpretations *and its use*, speak up.
- If you're an educator who realizes that many of your colleagues don't know squat about educational assessment, reach out—with colleague-convincing persuasiveness.

Now, I will present four op-ed essays that address four important flaws in the ways we currently employ educational tests. The messages these essays contain should be shared by all who believe that assess-ment's mission is to help instead of harm.

Publishers are typically reluctant to give away any of their wares. Yet, as a longtime ASCD member, I have acquired great respect for the association's efforts to improve schooling. Accordingly, I approached ASCD's publishing team with a request that this book's op-ed essays be made available to promote assessment literacy. To my delight but not my surprise, the publisher not only acceded to my wishes but also agreed to make the essays available online, thereby easing the promulgation task. Provided you include the copyright notice that appears at the bottom of each essay, ASCD grants you permission to distribute any or all of the chapter's four essays for the purpose of promoting assessment literacy. You'll find the downloadable and link-to-able versions at www.ascd.org/assessment-literacy.

I tried to make the essays short, and I attempted to write them without reliance on any technical talk. When I had to use ritzy-ditzy technical terms, I defined them on the fly. As written, these essays would be right at home in a local newspaper or a school or school district's monthly take-home (or digitally delivered) newsletter for parents. They might be circulated in advance of a faculty discussion focused on any of the assessment issues addressed in this book. Getting more specific, you might slip these essays to a colleague or two—openly or, if necessary, surreptitiously. It is my hope, frankly, that you will devote a few moments to thinking if there are any individuals, or groups of individuals, who would be—after reading one of these essays—not just better educators but, perhaps, *better human beings.*

Of course, I'd like *you* to read them, too, if only to enhance your ability to discuss these critical issues with others and keep any conversations about the benefits of assessment literacy alive.

OP-ED ESSAY NO. 1

USING THE WRONG TOOLS TO APPRAISE EDUCATIONAL QUALITY

W. James Popham
University of California, Los Angeles

Everyone wants children to be well educated. Accordingly, for more than a half-century, U.S. federal and state policymakers have been carefully trying to evaluate the quality of our nation's schools. Regrettably, the bulk of those evaluative efforts have failed miserably. That's because—with few exceptions—we have been using inappropriate tests to measure how well our students have learned.

Whether the focus of an evaluation is a state's entire school system or a particular school's effectiveness, the chief evidence that's employed to determine educational quality are students' scores on achievement tests, such as the annual state accountability tests required by federal law. Clearly, the quality and quantity of what students have learned in a school should be a dominant determiner of that school's success. Yet, almost all the tests we have currently chosen to evaluate our schools are flat-out wrong for this mission.

To do an accurate job of evaluating the quality of instruction within schools, a test must be "instructionally sensitive." In other words, it must be able to distinguish between well taught and badly taught students. However, if you were to review the technical documentation accompanying the standardized achievement tests we now employ to evaluate our schools, you would find there is no evidence—none at all—that these tests are up to that important assignment. Chiefly, this is because they are not measuring what we assume they are measuring.

This mismatch has historical roots. During World War I, U.S. Army officials commissioned the American Psychological Association to construct a written exam for recruits—an intelligence test to help identify potential lieutenants to lead the troops in France. They wanted an aptitude test to identify "the best of the best." The resultant test was called the "Army Alpha," and it was administered to about 1,750,000 Army recruits. It presented them with a set of verbal and numerical multiple-choice tasks, then sorted test-takers by comparing their total test scores; those who scored the highest were sent to officer training programs.

The Army Alpha was a hands-down winner, and much of its success stemmed from its design. The difficulty levels of items were expertly varied in a way that spread out the resulting scores so that fine-grained distinctions could be made among test-takers.

After the war, large-scale testing was introduced to U.S. education in the form of standardized achievement tests intended to measure students' mathematical, language, and social studies knowledge. These tests were built using the same score-spreading procedures pioneered during the Army Alpha's development. One crucial element of those procedures was the inclusion of numerous items that many test-takers would answer differently.

> In short, the tests used to evaluate schools often assess what students bring to school, not what they are taught once they arrive.

One of the very best ways to ensure that a test item produces varied responses is by linking the options in multiple-choice items to students' levels of affluence. If some answer-choices contain content that's likely to be familiar to children whose families' wealth provides more diverse experiences, those affluent students will get more correct answers than will their less affluent classmates. The Army Alpha included these kinds of items, and such items continue to be featured in the tests used to evaluate schools today. Although such affluence-slanted tests may do a crackerjack job of spreading out scores so that students can be compared, those tests tend to measure where a school's students are socioeconomically. In short, the tests used to evaluate schools often assess what students bring to school, not what they are taught once they arrive.

The work of America's educational test development firms is guided by the *Standards for Educational and Psychological Testing*, a joint publication of the three U.S. professional associations most concerned with educational assessment: the American Educational Research Association, the American Psychological Association, and the National Council on Measurement in Education. These standards carry great weight both in the field and in courtroom contests involving educational tests. The most recent edition of these standards, published in 2014, makes it unambiguously clear that when a test will be used for an important purpose—such as evaluating schools—there must be convincing evidence indicating that the test's score-based interpretations will be accurate, that is, valid. There must also be convincing evidence that the test has been designed to perform the job that we intend it to perform.

Because a test that's not instructionally sensitive can make weak schools look wonderful and stellar schools look shoddy, we dare not use instructionally insensitive tests to evaluate the quality of our schools. They are the wrong tools for the job. Better tests can be built for this crucial measurement mission. They must be.

OP-ED ESSAY NO. 2

PHONY ADVERTISING:
INSTRUCTIONALLY BENEFICIAL STANDARDIZED TESTS

W. James Popham
University of California, Los Angeles

It is a commonly held view, not only by educators, but also by the public, that standardized educational tests are a useful way to determine students' achievement levels and evaluate educators' effectiveness. Most people also believe standardized tests can also supply data that make a meaningful contribution to teachers' instruction—showing them where, for example, student knowledge is lacking and where additional teaching is required. Sadly, there is much more belief in the instructional virtues of standardized tests than there is evidence to support their use for instructional purposes.

To understand why the instructional promises of standardized educational tests outstrip their actual instructional contributions, we must first recognize an important reality about standardized tests. Whether it's an *achievement* test intended to measure students' current knowledge and skills, or an *aptitude* test employed to predict students' future academic performances, every standardized test is designed to spread out students' scores so that meaningful comparisons can be made among all who take it. It is this quest for *comparative* test scores that has led most standardized educational tests to be essentially useless for instruction. Let's see why.

What a teacher wants from a test is *actionable* information. In other words, when a teacher looks at a student's score on a test—or the collective test scores of many students—what that teacher wants to see are results that provide information about what to do next. For example, if certain students in an elementary teacher's class are struggling with subject-verb agreement, the teacher needs to know *which* students are having this trouble. Once those students are identified, the teacher can provide the strugglers with some targeted instruction about subject-verb agreement.

The instructional payoff of an educational test, whether it is a nationally standardized exam or a teacher-made classroom test, is that the test's results help teachers decide their best next steps. Yet, the inherently compara- tive mission of standardized educational tests meaningfully mucks up such tests' instructional contributions. A test focused chiefly on coming up with comparative scores is a test unable to make optimal contributions to a teacher's instructional decision making.

> The comparative thrust of standardized tests damages their instructional utility.

For any test to really help teachers make suitable "what-next" instructional decisions, that test's results need be reported at an appropriate "grain size." If the report's grain size is too broad, such as a test score indicating whether the stu- dent "can read with comprehension and understanding," the teacher can't discern where to aim next-step instruction. If the report's grain-size is too narrow, such as indicating whether a student answered *each* item correctly or incorrectly, the teacher becomes overwhelmed with too much undigested item-by-item informa- tion. Selecting an instructionally appropriate grain-size for a test clearly requires a Cinderella, "just right" decision.

Although it is *possible* to build standardized tests so that they describe students' performances at a suitable grain-size, this is incredibly difficult to accomplish. After all, these tests aim to measure students' mastery of a meaningful expanse of con- tent while also attempting spread out students' scores to permit comparisons. The comparative thrust of standardized tests—whether they are aimed at achievement or aptitude—simply beclouds the instructional utility of those tests.

Whether such falsely labeled "instructionally helpful" standardized tests are being peddled by commercial testing companies or by state and district education officials, users must not be swayed by their pro-instruction promises. Yes, if one deliberately sets out to provide educators with instructionally actionable next- step information, it is possible to construct tests that can help teachers teach better. But to do so effectively, a standardized test would need to downplay its traditional mission of providing results that compare test-takers.

In short, standardized tests purporting to help teachers provide improved instruction need to be accompanied by solid evidence that they do indeed serve that promised function. Absent this evidence, we must recognize the claims as what they are: sales pitches.

OP-ED ESSAY NO. 3
FORMATIVE ASSESSMENT: A MAGIC BULLET WAITING TO BE USED

W. James Popham
University of California, Los Angeles

Classroom formative assessment is a surefire way for teachers to improve their students' learning. Yet, despite massive evidence indicating that this test-based instructional approach works, too few teachers are currently using it. How come?

> Doubling the speed of students' learning is an aspiration worthy of pursuit.

Before digging into the potential reasons that formative assessment is being seriously underused in our nation's schools, let's agree on what formative assessment is. Consonant with the findings of an enormous amount of careful research conducted over the past four decades, most proponents of this assessment-illuminated instructional approach have agreed on a definition. Formative assessment is a planned process in which assessment-elicited evidence of students' status is used by teachers to adjust their ongoing instructional procedures or by students to adjust their current learning tactics. It is not a *kind* of test but a way of periodically employing tests to determine how well students have learned something and then looking at the test data to decide what classroom-based changes might support better learning.

Recent reviews of related research covering more than 4,000 investigations confirm that formative assessment works—big-time. One reviewer concluded that formative assessment, implemented well, can effectively *double* the speed of student learning. Certainly, doubling the speed of students' learning is an aspiration worthy of pursuit.

This is what the formative assessment process typically looks like. First, a teacher identifies an important *target curricular aim* that students should master. This can be a body of significant *knowledge,* such as the origin and meaning of the Bill of Rights, or an important *cognitive skill,* such as essay writing or hypothesis testing. Next, the teacher isolates key *building blocks* that students must definitely master on their way to achieving the target curricular aim. There might be only a handful of building blocks for a short-term instructional sequence but more such building blocks for extended-duration instruction. The entire sequence of instruction for promoting students' mastery of a given curricular aim might take just a few weeks, or it might require several months of instruction.

Toward the end of the instruction aimed at each building block, the teacher typically uses a teacher-made test or some other kind of performance evaluation to see if the students have mastered that skill or body of knowledge. If they have, *yahoo!* Instruction moves on to the next building block. But if they haven't, the teacher makes an adjustment in the planned instruction and tries a different approach to teach the tough-to-master building block. Based on the test data, students, too, might alter the ways they are trying to learn what's embodied in the building block.

Take a step back, and it becomes clear that formative assessment is a classic ends-means strategy—something human beings have been successfully employing since our earliest days on the planet. If a desired end (a target curricular aim) is not being attained by the means chosen to achieve it (a teacher's instructional approach or a student's learning approach), another means is selected to do the job. The habit of conducting ongoing checks on students' progress at key points and making adjustments when progress is stalling leads to more effective instruction and surer learning outcomes.

So why is something that works so wonderfully well, and has been highly touted in education circles for more than a decade, used by so few of today's teachers? Opinions about this vary, and mine may be miles off the mark. Yet, my suspicion is that many teachers who have tried to employ the formative assessment process simply found it to be too much trouble.

There is no denying the work involved. The process calls for carefully analyzing what a target curricular aim's enabling building blocks are, sequencing the building blocks in a logical learning progression, developing and administering assessments to determine students' building-block mastery, and determining from students' performances whether instructional adjustments are needed. And then, if adjustments are required, the teacher must figure out how to modify the planned instructional approach to better promote building-block mastery. It is easy to see why all this trouble can rapidly extinguish even a well-intentioned teacher's enthusiasm for formative assessment.

If I am correct about why formative assessment is underused, the potential solution strategy might be boiled down to one word: *prioritization*. If classroom teachers commit to using the formative assessment process only when pursuing a handful of their most important curricular aims, they can lower their risk of burning out, stick with the process, and reap the research-ratified rewards. When the learning-boosting power of formative assessment is trained on the highest-priority learning outcomes, everyone benefits—students especially.

OP-ED ESSAY NO. 4

THE MOST COST-EFFECTIVE WAY TO IMPROVE OUR SCHOOLS

W. James Popham
University of California, Los Angeles

Everyone wants our schools to be winners. What society would not want its schools to be as effective as possible? From an egalitarian perspective, we recognize education as a means of maximizing the inherent potential of our children. Aristotle once opined that the greatest metaphysical evil of all was an unattained potential. And Aristotle was smart.

From a more political perspective, members of a society are well served whenever their schools do a superb job of teaching children. That's because the cherished values that keep a society running—values like democracy, hard work, and responsibility—are more apt to be transmitted to the next generation when the society's schools are sailing along successfully. Clearly, it is in a society's self-interest to make sure its schools are effective.

And this is one reason why the United States has undertaken numerous initiatives over the years to strengthen the quality of public schooling. Some of those initiatives have worked; many have not. But there is currently one school improvement strategy sitting quietly on the shelf, as yet untried. It's an approach that could be, hands-down, the nation's *most cost-effective* way to improve our schools.

This economical school-improvement strategy is to enhance educators' *assessment literacy*—that is, to improve educators' understanding of the handful of fundamental assessment concepts and procedures that will support better instructional decision making. Once equipped with this insight, educators can share it with others who have a stake in the effectiveness of our schools—namely, parents, policymakers, and students themselves. Assessment literacy represents a little knowledge that, if used sensibly, can promote gobs of goodness in our schools. And the reason is simple: better instructional decisions lead to better-educated students.

> Assessment literacy represents a little knowledge that, if used sensibly, can promote gobs of goodness in our schools.

Obviously, there are other avenues to school improvement. We could double teachers' salaries so that tons of more talented young men and women would want to become teachers. We could dramatically reduce class sizes so that teachers could provide more one-on-one attention to individual students. Both approaches would likely boost school success, but both would be prohibitively expensive and difficult to enact in all communities.

In contrast, the promotion of educators' increased assessment knowledge costs a relative pittance. It can be done everywhere, and it can immediately inform test-based decisions that affect how our schools are operating, how our teachers are evaluated, and how our students are learning.

Consider that in almost all states and districts throughout the country, there are judgments being made about the instructional caliber of individual schools, and those judgments are based chiefly on students' performances on standardized achievement tests. But the tests being used for these evaluative purposes were never designed to perform that role, meaning test-based conclusions about which schools are good and which schools are bad are often baseless. Educators who are assessment literate can point out this fallacy and help put an end to such testing malpractice.

Well-designed tests—whether they target aptitude or achievement, are teacher-made and used in the classroom, or are standardized and required throughout an entire district—generate data that educators can use to infer what students know and can do. These insights allow educators to make comparisons among test-takers, improve ongoing instruction and learning, or evaluate instructional quality. But very, very few tests can generate data to support more than one of these missions at a time. Assessment-literate educators understand which kinds of tests to use for which purposes and how to interpret those test scores. Because the test-based conclusions they draw are apt to be accurate, the resulting actions they take to improve learning are more likely to be effective.

As another example, many of the standardized tests employed in schools are developed by commercial testing companies and sold to schools as a means of improving instruction. Yet, when students' test scores are returned to the schools, those results arrive in such excessively general terms that no one—not teachers, students, or parents—can figure out which instructional actions to take next. At the other extreme, some testing companies deliver score reports that provide a set of individual responses for every student, one item at a time, for teachers tasked with educating dozens if not hundreds of students every day. Making sense of such data is an overwhelming task, often sidelined by teachers' imperative to attend to student needs that are easier to diagnose. Assessment-literate educators know how to demand standardized tests that provide better, clearer, instructionally useful score reports.

If a sufficient number of assessment-literate educators call on educational officials to immediately halt today's harmful misuse of educational tests and reliance on unhelpful ones, those tests can be replaced by more suitable ones. But only educators who are themselves assessment literate will know whether the replacement tests are, in fact, suitable.

Some Final Words

Way back at the beginning of the book, I jabbered about judging a book by its cover or, in this instance, by its title: *Assessment Literacy for Educators in a Hurry*. Little did you realize, when reading those early words, that this title is, in a sense, a *trick* title, for its "in a hurry" notion represents two messages, not one.

For most of the book, I emphasized the reality that today's educators are terrifically time-pressed, so whatever assessment hijinks they choose to embark on must be truly time-efficient. To illustrate, I asked you to get comfy with only a half-dozen assessment understandings, not a hefty flock of such understandings. Today's educators are, as the title contends, a busy lot. Discretionary time is not abundant.

But there's a second sense in which the title's "in a hurry" notion applies, and I've waited until now to spring it on you. You see, if you have come to agree with me that increased assessment literacy could, for a relatively modest cost, bring about striking improvements in schooling, then you really ought to be eager and "in a hurry" to see some of the suggestions in this book implemented.

I hope that you're in a hurry to rescue schools, students, and colleagues from indefensible testing policies; that you're in a hurry to make better assessment-based instructional decisions to promote better learning; that you're in a hurry to disseminate the basics of informed assessment practice to all concerned clienteles; and, finally, that you're in a hurry to make things right instead of dwelling on what's wrong.

This concludes our time together. From my perspective, it has been good being with you. I've been constantly touting the importance of assessment literacy, and you have kindly put up with my haranguing on that issue. For one last time, allow me to assert the book's message with fervor aplenty:

> *The more that educators understand about the basics of educational assessment, the better decisions those educators will make about how best to teach their students.*

Now you and I are members of the very same club, the secret society I'll call the *Assessment Literacy Coven*. Well, if we're secret now, we won't be for much longer. We've got noise to make, information to share, wrongs to right, and children to help.

Coven Colleague, get out there and accomplish some assessment good!

REFERENCES

Ainsworth, L. (2015). *Common formative assessments, 2.0.* Thousand Oaks, CA: Corwin.

American Educational Research Association [AERA], American Psychological Association [APA], & National Council on Measurement in Education [NCME]. (2014). *Standards for educational and psychological testing.* Washington, DC: Author.

Anderson, L. W., & Bourke, S. F. (2000). *Assessing affective characteristics in the schools* (2nd ed.). Mahwah, NJ: Erlbaum.

Andrade, H. L., & Heritage, M. (2018). *Using formative assessment to enhance learning, achievement, and academic self-regulation.* New York: Routledge.

Black, P., & Wiliam, D. (1998a). Assessment and classroom learning. *Assessment in Education, 5*(1), 7–74.

Black, P., & Wiliam, D. (1998b). Raising standards through classroom assessment. *Phi Delta Kappan, 80*(2), 139–148.

Bloom, B., Englehart, M., Furst, E., Hill, W., & Krathwohl, D. (1956). *Taxonomy of educational objectives, Handbook I: Cognitive domain.* New York: David McKay.

Brookhart, S. M. (2013). *How to create and use rubrics for formative assessment and grading.* Alexandria, VA: ASCD.

Crooks, T. (1988). The impact of classroom evaluation practices on pupils. *Review of Educational Research, 58*(14), 438–481.

Duckworth, A. (2016). *Grit: The power of passion and perseverance.* New York: Simon & Schuster.

Hattie, J., & Yates, G. C. R. (2014). *Visible learning and the science of how we learn.* New York: Routledge.

Heritage, M. (2010). *Formative assessment: Making it happen in the classroom.* Thousand Oaks, CA: Corwin.

Likert, R. (1932). A technique for the measurement of attitudes. *Archives of Psychology, 140,* 1–55.

Piaget, J. (1978). *Success and understanding.* Cambridge, MA: Harvard University Press.

Popham, W. J. (2008). *Transformative assessment.* Alexandria, VA: ASCD.

Popham, W. J. (2011). *Transformative assessment in action.* Alexandria, VA: ASCD.

Popham, W. J. (2017a). *Classroom assessment: What teachers need to know* (8th ed.). Boston: Pearson.

Popham, W. J. (2017b). Understanding the test. *American School Board Journal, 204*(3), 22–26.

Sadler, D. R. (1989). Formative assessment and the design of instructional strategies. *Instructional Science, 18,* 119–144.

Scriven, M. (1967). The methodology of evaluation. In R. W. Tyler, R. M. Gagne, & M. Scriven (Eds.), *Perspectives of curriculum evaluation, Volume I* (pp. 39–83). Chicago: Rand-McNally.

Stiggins, R., & Chappuis, J. (2017). *An introduction to student-involved assessment for learning* (7th ed.). Boston: Pearson.

Tyson, N. D. (2017). *Astrophysics for people in a hurry.* New York: Norton.

Wiliam, D. (2007/2008, December–January). Changing classroom practices. *Educational Leadership, 65*(4), 36–42.

Wiliam, D. (2011). *Embedded formative assessment.* Bloomington, IN: Solution Tree.

Wolfe, P. (2010). *Brain matters: Translating research into classroom practice* (2nd ed.). Alexandria, VA: ASCD.

INDEX

The letter *f* following a page number denotes a figure.

ABOUT THE AUTHOR

W. James Popham is a professor emeritus in the UCLA Graduate School of Education and Information Studies. He has spent the bulk of his educational career as a teacher, first of English and social studies in a small, eastern Oregon high school and later at UCLA, where he spent nearly 30 years teaching instructional methods to prospective teachers and graduate courses in evaluation and measurement.

At UCLA, Dr. Popham won several distinguished teaching awards, and he was recognized in January 2000 by *UCLA Today* as one of UCLA's top 20 professors of the 20th century (a *full-length* century, he notes, unlike the current abbreviated one). In 1992, he took early retirement from UCLA, influenced in no small part by the free parking guaranteed to emeritus professors.

Dr. Popham has published more than 200 journal articles and more than 30 books, many of which have been translated into Spanish, Portuguese, Arabic, French, Farsi, Chinese, Japanese, Korean, and Canadian. His most recent books include *Classroom Assessment: What Teachers Need to Know*, 8th ed. (2017), *The ABCs of Educational Testing: Demystifying the Tools That Shape Our Schools* (2017), *Evaluating America's Teachers: Mission Possible?* (2013), *Mastering Assessment* (2011), *Everything School Leaders Need to Know About Assessment* (2010), *Transformative Assessment* (2008), and *Assessment for Educational Leaders* (2006).

Dr. Popham was elected to the presidency of the American Educational Research Association (AERA) in 1978 and was the founding editor of AERA's quarterly journal, *Educational Evaluation and Policy Analysis*. A fellow of the Association, he has attended every AERA annual meeting since 1958. He is inordinately compulsive.

In 1968, Dr. Popham established IOX Assessment Associates, a research and development group that created statewide student achievement tests for a dozen states. He personally passed all those tests, largely because of his unlimited access to the tests' answer keys.

He received the National Council on Measurement in Education Award for Career Contributions to Educational Measurement in 2002, and from 2009 to 2017 he served as a member of the National Assessment Governing Board. In 2014, he received an honorary doctorate of public service from his alma mater, the University of Portland in Oregon.

Dr. Popham's complete 50-page, single-spaced vita is available upon request. He warns that it is really dull reading.

Related ASCD Resources: Assessment

At the time of publication, the following resources were available (ASCD stock numbers in parentheses):

PD Online® Courses

Designing Assessments for Higher-Order Thinking (#PD15OC008M)
Formative Assessment: Deepening Understanding (#PD11OC101M)

Print Products

Fast and Effective Assessment: How to Reduce Your Workload and Improve Student Learning by Glenn Pearsall (#118002)

Grading Smarter, Not Harder: Assessment Strategies That Motivate Kids and Help Them Learn by Myron Dueck (#114003)

How to Make Decisions with Different Kinds of Student Assessment Data by Susan M. Brookhart (#116003)

Mastering Formative Assessment Moves: 7 High-Leverage Practices to Advance Student Learning by Brent Duckor and Carrie Holmberg (#116011)

The Perfect Assessment System by Rick Stiggins (#117079)

Transformative Assessment by W. James Popham (#108018)

Using Data to Focus Instructional Improvement by Cheryl James-Ward, Douglas Fisher, Nancy Frey, and Diane Lapp (#113003)

For up-to-date information about ASCD resources, go to www.ascd.org. You can search the complete archives of *Educational Leadership* at www.ascd.org/el.

For more information, send an email to member@ascd.org; call 1-800-933-2723 or 703-578-9600; send a fax to 703-575-5400; or write to Information Services, ASCD, 1703 N. Beauregard St., Alexandria, VA 22311-1714 USA.